AJ,

Congrats on your

NPMA Post.

AC Lahyer

"Start here - but only if you want to grow and replicate your business and thrive in times of disruption. AC (or The Five Keys to Pattern Success) takes the mystery out of scaling any business while creating profits every step of the way."

–Tom Ziglar,
CEO of Zig Ziglar Corporation

AC Lockyer has a head for business and a heart for people. His new book, The Five Keys to Pattern Success, captures both of these important qualities and provides a framework for building a life that is much more meaningful and fulfilling. More importantly, his message is focused on helping people build a legacy that positively impacts others now and for generations to come. His advice is practical and can be put to work immediately in your life.

–Roy Reid, APR, CPRC
AdventHealth

"The greatest life lesson I've ever learned is to get around successful people and learn what made them successful. AC has a long track record of success in business and in life. In this book, he has laid out his pattern of success for you to follow. Read this book and you'll have the roadmap to success"

–Howard Partridge,
Phenomenal Business Coaching

"In his book, The Five Keys to Pattern Success, AC Lockyer gives a great explanation of steps to success that have worked for him in his highly successful business. This simple-to-understand, yet highly effective formula will help you take your business to the next level. AC's book is easy-to-read, and the content is easy-to-practice. I've known him for more than three decades, and have had a front row seat to how he's used these steps in his own business. Not finding something that would help him, he created his own formula, The Five Keys to Pattern Success, and now he's described it in great detail in this book, making it easy for YOU to understand and use. He's masterfully laid out what he believes are the five key components to enable you to experience success again and again. AC's taught it to hundreds of entrepreneurs around the world, and now he's making it available to you! Why not put these steps to work for you?"

–Dan Holland,
CEO Droplet International

THE FIVE KEYS TO
PATTERN
SUCCESS

REPLICATE SUCCESS AT WILL IN YOUR
PERSONAL AND BUSINESS LIFE

AC LOCKYER

CONTENTS

The Fifth Key – SYSTEMIZE

The Locks, The Keys, The Order

INTRODUCTION

"There is nothing new under the sun."
~King Solomon

Every idea, every thought, every system has its roots in an idea, thought, or system that came before yours. Nothing is truly unique. Nothing is actually original. Rarely is any business system so very revolutionary. Everything is simply rehashed.

Being a musician, to me, ideas, thoughts, and systems are a song. This book for me is the opportunity to get these songs out of my mind and into a medium that others can enjoy and maybe even emulate. Seeing another appreciate your song so much as to play (cover it) or even stylize it brings everything in life full circle. As a musician, the greatest compliment is to see another perform your song.

The biggest fear a musician has is to die with a song in their head that they never were able to share with the world. This book is my effort to get my song (business systems) out to you. My hope is for you to use these in your business, to make your business sing. To cover my song. Then by that, you can achieve all of your life's goals and dreams.

The great theologian Ozzy Osborne said it well,

*"There are only 88 keys on a piano.
Someone is bound to eventually write
a song that sounds like yours."*
~Ozzy Osborne

Now, I am sure Ozzy would have taken great offense to someone using the opening riff of "Crazy Train" and claiming it was theirs. However, Ozzy understood a riff of 12 notes in three measures, at the rate of 136 bpm, played in the first position, on the 6th string of a guitar ... there are simply only so many combinations. The point Ozzy was making was "do not get bent out of shape, music is the universal language. Celebrate innovation, but don't get caught up in the ownership.

That being said, I do believe and am passionate about my songs (systems). I feel wholeheartedly that they will revolutionize your business. I know now, from years of coaching other service businesses worldwide, that these systems work, all of the time. These Five Keys to Pattern Success that I will introduce you to will absolutely alter the direction of your life and help you to be more successful than your wildest imagination ... if you take them to heart and EXECUTE the pattern.

Patterns are everywhere. Obviously, in music, they are apparent. A pattern of notes becomes a melody, the melody becomes the hook, the hook is added to the chorus and now you have a song. Patterns also exist in sports. In 2006 I exploited patterns in fishing to become a national champion. Patterns also exist in business. Marketing and sales depend on and exploit patterns in buying habits and the patterns of spending exhibited in human beings that are eerily similar to the patterns exhibited in fish and animals.

CHAPTER 1

THE GENESIS

As of the writing of this book, I have ownership, stock, or interest (different from ownership) in over 200 businesses in nine countries. That is scary-amazing to me because it was only ten years ago I went completely broke, down to my last $250. This was all due to my immaturity in business, bad decisions, and an unbelievably painful family business breakup. Today, I am a blessed child of God, living my life to glorify Him, investing the talents He gave me every day, to hear from my master one day, "Well done, good and faithful servant."

I am a third-generation service business entrepreneur. My father is an entrepreneur; my grandfather was an entrepreneur. In fact, a Lockyer male has not worked for another person for over 100 years. I did not initially want to go the route of entrepreneurship. Honestly, my dream was to be a long-haired lead singer in a heavy metal rock and roll band. Obviously, that did not happen.

What did happen is that this Florida boy ended up going to college in West Texas. Actually, to get a ministry degree. That's its own story. Seemingly, I ended up not quite being college material. However, while at that college, I met the girl of my dreams. A cute little red-headed, yellow rose of Texas rocked my world, and I fell in deep.

Once I was done with college (it rather being done with me), I decided to move back to Florida. Before that, I knew I wanted to spend the rest of my life with the redhead. I proposed to her, and she accepted. I then packed up my worldly possessions and my cat and moved home to Florida.

While en route back home, I would stop and check in with my parents via a pay phone. Yes, these were the days before cell phones. I was telling my parents about my redhead, how I wanted to make a life with her, and how much I was in love. That's when I asked my dad about pitching me an idea for a business I could start so I could support my new love and start a life together.

Now, my father was a well-known local service business owner, involved in the community and our local church. Many came to him for business advice, and he freely gave it. Several times, he spawned ideas for businesses for young men in our church after layoffs and life changes so they could become entrepreneurs and support their families. He would help with the service, the name, and even coach these budding entrepreneurs, helping them get on their feet. I was not unlike many of the young men my dad had helped, so of course, I reached out to him on one of these calls and asked him to pitch me an idea for my business.

It happens that our preferred "family" painter had just finished painting my parent's home. While prepping the house for painting, our family painter had pressure washed the exterior of the home. In the process of that cleaning, he also jumped up on the roof and pressure washed away the black, ugly stains that had covered the roof and tarnished the beauty of the shingles. My dad explained the process and told me, "It really made the whole house look great. Seems to me this would be a great business to develop. You wouldn't need to have x-ray vision to see if a homeowner had a Kirby vacuum in the closet. You will be able to see right away if they need their roof cleaned or not. Easy to find a target prospect."

You know what's flooding my mind now? I am about 12 hours from home, ready to get married to my cute little redhead, and raring to build a name for myself. All I could think about all the rest of the way home was roof cleaning. I mean "think" like Bubba in Forest Gump talked about shrimp when Forest and he were in Vietnam dreaming about buying a shrimp boat. I was looking at every roof as I drove east on I-10, dreaming about the types of roofs, pondering how to reach my customers, thinking about how to build cleaning systems, etc. Truly obsessed with it.

Now, if you ask my father today why he pitched the idea of roof cleaning to me back in 1991, his story is a bit different than mine. My dad knows I am afraid of heights. He knew I didn't like working outside. He knew it would be physical work. He tells everyone he was just trying to pitch to me the scariest, dirtiest, hard work business idea he could muster in an effort to drive me back into college and finish my degree. He underestimated how "ready" I was to get married and make babies. Have you seen my cute little redhead?

Well, now I am a roof cleaner. I have started a roof cleaning business. However, the same demons that plagued me through high school and college were stumbling blocks in my business as well. The truth is I have two diagnosed clinical mental differences.

Early in elementary school, I had "ants in my pants," and in the 70s, ADHD was not a diagnosed disorder. My next-door neighbor, Bertha Shouldice, worked at Barry University in Miami Beach, Florida. They had launched a program trying to identify learning differences, largely in boys, affecting performance in school environments. My neighbor asked my parents if it was okay for her to take me afternoons, after school, to participate in this program. I was in the second grade.

The program found that mostly boys (and sometimes girls) had a condition where they were not unintelligent but rather bored and distracted easily. This was an early understanding of ADHD. Tests and studies were done on our group, and many of these findings were passed on to our teachers so they could help us adjust to a school-based learning environment.

This all sounded great. You would certainly think that tests, studies, and identifying learning differences to help a young boy do better in school would only be positive. For me, it was quite the opposite.

These findings revealed to my teachers who I was and how I was made up as an individual, and this information became part of my permanent record. For years, I had a string of frustrated teachers, pushing me for results and always telling me the same thing over and over, "You could do so much more, have much better grades if only you would just apply yourself." The expectations were raised for me dramatically, and I did not know why.

I remember it wasn't until I was in seventh grade, middle school. I had a WONDERFUL social studies teacher who sat me down as I was failing her class and was almost doomed to repeat the seventh grade. (I had already repeated the third grade.) She pulled my record and opened it up to me. All of my report cards, all of my teachers' notes, everything on me up to that point as a student were in that file.

She then pulled out a single report and put her finger on a number. A number seemed so innocuous. How could one number mean so much? She was so excited and so frustrated all at once. I had seen that look before on several teachers' faces who had preceded her.

A number, three digits, that supposedly said so much about my potential. That number 159 was the first time I had ever seen it or really understood it. She immediately compared me to Albert Einstein and others, but this time, the look of frustration turned to compassion as she told me she was going to move me out of my regular social studies class into an AP social studies class. I did not know what AP meant. She explained that it meant advanced placement.

ADHD is like having a mind like a supercharged, high output race car engine that someone has screwed up the firing order on the spark plug wires. Yes, those with ADHD diagnoses are more likely to be geniuses, but the application of the horsepower is off somewhere. In the past, teachers would only see that number and have such high hopes of having another little Einstein in their class; however, in reality, I was much more closely associated with Eddie Munster.

My social studies teacher explained that she thought I would do better if I was in a higher-paced, work at my own pace, student-led learning environment. You know what I did? I earned my first A ever in my school career. From that day forward until I graduated, I never received less than a B in social studies. Now math, that was a different story.

As an adult, I still struggled in my business. My ADHD was bothering me, and I was on medication. Through counseling, I was encouraged to go and see a psychologist.

All my life, I would get obsessed with some aspects of my life and leave others to flounder and fail. Through testing and study, I added another diagnosis to my already cluttered mind. I was diagnosed with OCD, obsessive-compulsive disorder. Do you know what someone's life looks like that has ADHD and OCD together? An obsessive that cannot pay attention to their projects.

I only tell you this because we all have learning differences/circumstances to overcome. We all have unrealized talents. We all have defeats in our story. I had a mixed bag of all these that were dragging my business down. I had to compensate and compensate quickly.

Compensate. Now, that is a wonderful and miraculous word. Compensate, like driving a car or a boat. When you are on the wrong path, just steer back onto the right path … COMPENSATE. It was such a revelation. I needed to either get really, really good at understanding when I was on or off the right path, or create margins, borders, or bumpers (systems) that kept me on the right path in business and in life. *Compensate*, to me, became *systemize*, and we were off to the races.

Systemizing a business was so freeing for me. Creating business systems helped me keep track of my score, how I was doing, if I had a good day. I would work the system like a mathematical equation, and BOOM! I had a REPLICABLE result.

CHAPTER 2

THE FIVE KEYS

I have a life system that has absolutely led to my success over and over. It is a simple system that I can teach you. With this system, you can win over and over in your life and replicate success. The five keys are simple and gravitational.

BE DELIBERATE
EXECUTE
ANALYZE
REPLICATE
SYSTEMIZE

For many years, I have used my hand to remind me of this system, as the illustration here shows. Notice the gap between the thumb (Be DELIBERATE) and the index finger (EXECUTE)? It is the widest gap on our hand. It hit me many years later why that gap is there in my easy-to-remember keys on my hand. I knew, for many, having an idea or a plan was much easier than EXECUTING that idea or plan. Most get caught up in that gap between DELIBERATE and EXECUTE, and they never see their dreams to fruition.

I did not realize it until I was at a Howard Partridge, Phenomenal Products convention that this existed or what it was called. Howard was speaking on failure to implement. Later he wrote a book on this concept. Howard explained that many of us have dreams and goals. We have plans for our businesses and for our families, but rarely do we follow through on these dreams or plans. He described this as *Failure to Implement*.

I then realized why the gap between the thumb and index finger was significant. Being DELIBERATE was having a dream or a plan. Actually, EXECUTING was the biggest struggle in life. IMPLEMENTATION was the obstacle or chasm that most goals and dreams were lost to, so very few people ever move onto EXECUTION because of the lack of implementation. Thanks to Howard Partridge, I was able to identify this and add it to The Five Keys model.

These five words have a deeper meaning. They are five words that can aid in or direct every decision or goal in your life, personal or business. Five words that are disruptive and divisional in culture and society. Five words that, when marinated into your thoughts, can be transformational. While others around you seem to struggle with life, you will take on challenges with ease and seem to have a charmed life.

In this book, I am going to break down these five keys into five sections. In each section, three chapters will help you grasp the concepts of this easy system. I will start out on the concept of each Key. Then tell a story from my life on how I practically used that Key, either from my personal or business life. Then round off the third chapter by sharing one of my systems for making that Key work practically and giving thought and advice on how you can implement that Key into your life.

I will teach you how to identify patterns and how to capitalize on those patterns over and over again. Life is full of REPLICABLE patterns. Knowing how to identify and even come to depend on these patterns will help you achieve your life's goals.

For a time in my life, I was a professional tournament fisherman. In fact, in 2006, my fishing partner Thresher Klier and I achieved one of my life goals (On the Bucket List) and won the Redfish Tour National Championship. It was our rookie season.

AC and his partner, Thresher Klier after winning the
2006 Redfish Tour National Championship

Fishing, though thought to be based upon luck, is certainly based on skill. Many will say phrases like "The fish were not biting today" or "They just were not hungry today" to describe how successful a fishing trip had been. I ask you, do fish ever stop eating? When was the last time you stopped eating? Do you not have to eat every day? Fish do as well.

The fact is fish, like people, eat several times a day. (Stay with me here even if you do not like fishing. Roll with this comparison. It will make sense to you.) Yes, their appetite may be off now and then. They may have a craving for a particular food just like we do.

Just like you and I, even when our appetite is suppressed due to weather, emotion, illness, or stress, there is surely something on your list of favorites that will soothe even the deepest despair and heighten your cravings. For me, that is chocolate. It does not matter what mood I am in and how long ago I have eaten, tempt me with chocolate, and I'm in.

Fish are the same way. However, you must figure out where they are, when they are hungry, and what they are craving at that particular moment. Learning to anticipate or even depend on these variables is called establishing a pattern.

So how do you accomplish that? You use the Five Keys to Pattern Success.

How do you find and marry your wife? The Five Keys.

How do you develop a successful marketing campaign? The Five Keys.

How do you revolutionize an entire industry? The Five Keys.

How do you build a multi-million dollar business? The Five Keys.

You are five steps away from accomplishing your goals. Five steps away from your life's work. Five steps away from a championship. Five steps away from peace and stress elimination.

I have used these same Five Keys to accomplish seemingly impossible successes in my own life. Seemingly unreachable goals in a short period of time. Like winning The Redfish Tour National Championship our rookie season by using these Five Keys to create a system for replicating success over and over.

AC while fishing the Redfish Tour

Establishing these patterns for me has led people to think that I lead a charmed life. In reality, I am only putting to use my God-given time, talent, opportunities, and relationships. You, like I, have an ample blessing of all of those above. Acting on these blessings does take some work.

Nothing admirable is ever easily accomplished and success rarely ever goes uncriticized. When you start to focus on this system — and by that, I mean start having success in your own life — you will be criticized. Success is but a mirror. To some, it reflects (and thereby confirms) the positive steps they are taking to have success in life.

To others, it reflects the missteps and laziness that have led to their demise. Once you start replicating success repeatedly in your life, your peer group may need to be upgraded. You will stand out, and you will be attacked.

Let us go on this discovery journey to your Five Keys to Pattern Success in your life.

KEY NUMBER ONE -
BE DELIBERATE

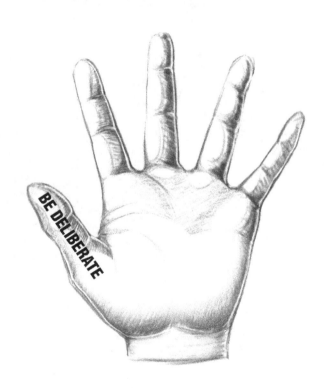

CHAPTER 3

MOVING WITH PURPOSE

I find it interesting how we define words today. Words do not seem to mean what they used to. Cultural agents with agendas hijack words and redefine them so there is no longer a standard, no longer accountability, or if they cannot redefine a word, they demonize the word and say it is judgmental. In life, you must have anchor points — unmovable beliefs that cannot be convoluted or distorted. Words that do not blow back and forth in the wind. Let us look at the word DELIBERATE.

DELIBERATE
Done consciously and with intention.

DELIBERATELY
In a careful and unhurried way.

DELIBERATION
Long and careful consideration or discussion.

I want you to merge all three of these uses or definitions to describe your goal setting or dream casting process.

OUR DELIBERATE DEFINITION
To move consciously with intention in a careful and unhurried way, giving long and careful consideration to your plans.

You need to have a plan. Dreams can be plans. Set goals. You cannot reach a destination without a plan or a map. You will not hit a target you do not aim for. In my life, it has been so especially important to stop the busyness of life and plan out the next season of my life.

Often, my best time to work things out in my head (drain my brain) is on a road trip. I do not understand completely why my most productive times are on the road. It might be because of my learning differences.

The ADHD parts of my brain get distracted by the road. The white noise of the wind. The hum of the tires. The occasional distractions of the sights, sounds, and smells as I'm driving along. Something just abruptly and suddenly clicks, and my creative juices start to flow. I start to have ideas, design assemblies, dream about the future. It all just seems to come into focus on the road.

I encourage you to find out what your sweet spot is for dreaming. If you do not dream, you will not grow.

AC and his 1960 Ford Truck, Blue Belle

Proverbs 29:18
Where there is no vision, the
people will perish.

To be an entrepreneur, at least a successful one, you need to have a bit of a visionary in you. You need to see your business path clearly. A great leader effectively communicates their vision to their team.

Life is a chain of choices. There are no good or bad choices; choices are benign. Results are good, bad, or indifferent. Every person is the sum of the choices they have made. The results define them. If you are going to be judged by the results of the choices you have made, wouldn't you want to have a higher plane of ownership in those choices?

What I mean by a higher plane of ownership is that you decide to have more control over the circumstances that shape the outcome of your decisions. For instance, you can wake up in the morning, make the decision to have a positive attitude, and enjoy your day. However, if the company you keep are negative, unhappy people, then that decision would most likely not yield a good result. The company you keep, your friends, family, and co-workers would influence you and thereby affect the result of your decision.

If you hang out with positive thinkers, happy souls that are optimistic, well then, it is easy to make a DELIBERATE decision to have a positive attitude for the day. Getting control of your personal influencers and surroundings helps your personal decisions go well. Likewise, getting control of your business influencers and surroundings will make your business decisions go well too.

Whom you align yourself with will affect your business decisions more than opportunity, talent, skills, or business acumen combined. Being DELIBERATE in picking business partners, mentors, or associations will have a profound effect on the success of your business. Finding positive and meaningful customer relationships, supplier relationships, and coaching relationships is a first priority task when growing your business.

I really enjoy blessing suppliers with business from my companies. I take a great deal of pride from using local suppliers and seeing them prosper from the business I give them. It is one of the things that gives my companies as well as myself purpose on this earth. The world is round; what goes around comes around. If you do not bless other businesses and suppliers around you, then do not expect that same courtesy when people choose to do, or not to do, business with you.

I do have a personal rule however that guides these supplier relationships.

The relationship must be mutually beneficial, and the flow of good results must flow both ways.

If I decide to outsource a material or assembly for one of my businesses and a supplier is doing a great job producing a quality product and keeping up with our demand, then we both win. If I find myself spending a lot of time and energy firming that supplier up or covering for their mistakes, then I may need to find another supplier.

You see if I make a bad decision, fail, or produce an inferior product myself, then I can take the hit and strive to make it better. However, the one thing I really do not like is taking the hit for a supplier, or damaging my brand's reputation, for a product I did not make.

This leads me often to vertically integrate and pull that product or process in-house for us to produce ourselves. You can clearly see how my desire to make a good decision was influenced by my supplier for the good or the bad. Choose your suppliers carefully.

Another place you can be DELIBERATE in making a great decision for your business, but the outcome goes horribly wrong, is in how you surround yourself with the right customers. DELIBERATELY deciding to onboard only the best of customers is very much like choosing friends. If you choose the wrong customers, they will drag you and your business down.

Having great customers should come hand-in-hand with having a great product. This is not always the case. You can have the world's best product but keep picking loser customers much in the same way a talented, beautiful girl picks loser boyfriends.

You often pick loser customers because you do not value yourself. Business esteem is just as important as self-esteem. You need to see that your product is talented and beautiful. Just as that wonderful girl needs to raise her standard in the men she is choosing, so must you in the customers you choose. Knowing who you are looking for in a customer is important and one of the most DELIBERATE things you can do for your business.

There is a phrase in marketing called The Avatar Customer. This is where you have a whiteboard session describing who your ideal customer is. Their income level, their gender, their age group, likes, passions, and alike go into developing The Avatar of your customer. Do you know who your Avatar Customer is, or are you just trying to sell to anyone who will bite?

Being DELIBERATE in all of these first steps of your business or personal life will help you build the best foundation for great results. Without this foundation, you cannot move on to the other four keys. Being DELIBERATE, having a dream, and putting a plan to paper are all essential bedrock moves you must make before having a successful life.

CHAPTER 4

OF RED HAIR

In each of these five sections that profile your Five Keys to Pattern Success, I will share a story of my life in which that key was present. These are the stories I share when I am speaking at various conventions and education opportunities. These are the stories I look back upon fondly in my life and see clearly how these disciplines shaped me.

If you know much about me, then you know I have a wife that I love eternally, a woman who is my true soul mate and who completes me in every way. How we met and dated is somewhat the typical college sweetheart story, but what you may not know is that she was a bet. Yes. A challenge, a good old-fashioned prodding from my college roommates that has a funny story behind it.

As you may know, when you are in college, especially a Christian college, one of your goals is likely not academic. For many, one goal is to date and find their future spouse.

For me, this was basically my number one goal. You see I did go to college to get a degree. I did want to become a pastor and go into the ministry. I did want to achieve the goal of being the first Lockyer to ever go to and graduate from college. However, I was on the hunt.

At Abilene Christian University, I was in a dorm where the rooms were configured in suites. One entrance would lead to a hall with a single group bathroom and four dorm rooms where a total of eight male students would live for the semester.

When you put eight man-boys in the same domicile, you know the conversation is going to eventually lead to girls. What is your type? Who do you think is cute? Do you want to get married young or live it up a bit before settling down? I was always the settle down and start a family kind of guy.

When the conversation focused on "What is your type?" I had a type. I wanted a girl like good-ole mom. I wouldn't say it was a case of Oedipus Syndrome. (I did not have the hots for my mom.) However, for whatever reason, I really was attracted to genuine redheads. (Yes, my mom is a redhead).

Well, in a group of man-boys, that leads to all kinds of discussions, as you can imagine. After all of the teasing and innuendo, one of my suite-mates chimed in and said, "So you like redheads? You mean girls like...," and a list began to be compiled.

Firstly, we had to define a true redhead. No bottle reds would do. (I called these fakers.) A true redhead has real red hair, auburn, red, or strawberry. True redheads have alabaster skin and freckles. True redheads have feisty personalities. So, after some jovial discussion, we began to cull and refine the list of eligible redheads at ACU.

Now the list got to be fairly large. I had not truly realized that a Christian university in West Texas would be such a hot bed for ginger goddesses. The list settled in at 33 young flaxen ladies. (Which, by the way, is my lucky number and the number I raced under when I did BMX racing as a kid.)

Once the list was complete the man-boys jumped at the next logical conclusion. A bet. A dare. A conquest. It roared out of one suite-mate's mouth, "I bet you can't date each girl on that list in one semester!"

Okay, the gauntlet was thrown down. The challenge was set forth. Now we had to define the ground rules. Firstly, what was a date? Was a date purely romantic? Can it be a get-to-know-you event, like coffee? Can it be in a group of people like a group date or a double date? Could it be a church date? Could it be going to chapel together during the school day? (At ACU, we had a daily chapel assembly with the entire student body.) What truly defined a "DATE"?

Once the list was finalized and the ground rules were set, I took on the challenge and set off to date every redhead on the list.

Now there were many beautiful redheads at ACU. True stunners that had the look. However, I quickly realized that my future wife might be on this list. At least if everything worked out right. I might just have, with the help of my posse, systemized the likely approach that would lead to wedded bliss and the life and family I always wanted.

Thinking about this, I started to realize that beauty is skin deep, and I might have to spend a lifetime with one of these goddesses. While in thought with this, I came up with my own personal criteria for my future Mrs. Lockyer.

Okay, okay, okay. I know this is supposed to be a business systems book. I get it. I know this is not a romance novel. However, this is important stuff. You know, if you marry wrong and become un-equally yoked in life, life may not go well for you.

Your life partner in almost all cases can make or break you in the rest of your life's endeavors. Getting this right, like many other decisions in life, is important. Being DELIBERATE in this story of how I found my wonderful wife is absolutely a perfect analogy of how I attack decisions and goal setting in my business life as well. So, you must stay with me and endure the rest of this story.

Here we go. The future Mrs. Lockyer needed to be beautiful, of course. That goes without saying. However, if I was going to spend the rest of my life with her, she needed to have a brain. I would need a woman of great character (Proverbs 31). A woman with whom I could have deep conversations. A woman with whom I could do ministry. Also, being a third-generation entrepreneur, I would need a woman who could help me be the best I could be in my business.

I do not like rail-thin ladies. I am not athletically built myself. I wanted a woman who was a woman. Who could work alongside me. Play alongside me. Granted, I am esthetically driven. Yes, she needed to look great in a dress. (In my future wife's style, a Leslie Luck dress.)

I preferred that the future Mrs. Lockyer look great in blue jeans too. Make-up was to be minimal. I liked pale alabaster skin with freckles and natural beauty. No dishonest beauty here. I wanted to wake up every morning to natural beauty, inside and out.

The future Mrs. Lockyer needed to love God. I have always been a very spiritual person. I believe I have been placed here on this earth with a purpose. I participate in God's plan daily, and I wanted my wife to be as spiritually driven as I was.

This woman would need to be the mother to my children. Love and care for them. Bring them up in the ways of the Lord. Teach them to be respectful and honest. Lead our children to become gracious people who love and serve others. Be others-centered and make a difference in the lives of the people she touched.

I wanted to grow old with this person and experience life with her. I didn't want her to be too serious. I wanted to have fun. I wanted to joke, horse around, play slug bug, and be real. I wanted to grow old with this person and have breakfast on the back porch every morning. I wanted to live a long life together and eventually die sometime after our 50th anniversary and no sooner.

I know you're thinking, "WOW, AC! That's quite a description of who you wanted as your Mrs. Lockyer." And you would be right. Literally, that would seem to be an impossible list. However, I knew what I wanted and set out to date every young redheaded lady on that list to see if the future Mrs. Lockyer could be found.

Now you should know, I think my dorm suitemates soon forgot about the list. It was a fun night and ensuing weeks after, but the novelty wore off, much like what happens to the plans we have in our lives or vocations. Not for me though. I pushed on.

Number 13 on the list was a girl from West Texas. A tallish girl at 5'8". Medium build in a size 6 dress. BIG West Texas 1980s auburn hair (with a bow). Alabaster skin, freckles, and blue eyes. With a personality and grit like being pistol-whipped by a drunk cowboy. I fell hopelessly head over heels in love with her.

We went out on a few dates, and it was a bit casual with low expectations at first until ... one Sunday after church, I was in the student center getting ready to go eat at THE WORLD-FAMOUS BEAN cafeteria. I was chatting with a friend when someone came up behind me and covered my eyes with their hands. It was a girl; I could smell her perfume. Her hands were smooth and warm. "Guess who?" she said as she held her hands over my eyes. She removed her hands, and I spun around and gazed upon the beautiful Ms. Karen.

Auburn hair, all curled and teased, and a bow atop. Beautiful alabaster skin and blue eyes. Dressed in a white with black trim and polka dots Leslie Luck dress and high heels. It was a moment in time that still brings me to tears today.

At that exact moment, I knew I needed to stop with the crazy bet and go back and close the deal with this girl. I could totally see myself spending the rest of my life with this flaxen goddess and making her my queen.

We dated about one and a half years, and on June 13 (yes, the number Karen was on the infamous redheads of ACU list), 1992, we became husband and wife and started our crazy life together. Karen always likes to point out (seemingly disgusted, but she loves it) that she was a BET, a CHALLENGE, that she was not #1 on the list but rather #13. However, it worked out pretty well for both of us.

AC and his bride, Karen, at their wedding in 1992

Looking back on this story, is there any wonder I married a redhead? Is there any wonder, as of the publishing of this book, we are celebrating our 30th anniversary together? Any wonder we have two wonderful adult, well-adjusted children? Is it a mystery we own several businesses TOGETHER and work alongside each other every day and have not killed each other as of yet? It was all part of a plan. A dream, A DELIBERATE system put into place to guide the process that ended up in true success.

I knew what I wanted, and with the help of my suitemates, I put the plan to paper and EXECUTED the plan to perfection. You too can have personal and business victories like this if you live DELIBERATELY. Dream, plan, and EXECUTE. You will see it all work out, but it starts with being DELIBERATE.

CHAPTER 5

THE MILLION-DOLLAR MAP

Sometimes, it is difficult to envision the path forward in your business. Putting together a business plan is the typically accepted way to plot the course for a successful business. However, often the entrepreneur simply cannot put his vision into writing.

A business plan can take many forms and functions. It can be in the written word, or it can be very visual in nature with pictorial benchmarks, goals, and data that for some is very hard to digest in plain writing, paragraph by paragraph. I use a very visual exercise called The Million-Dollar Map.

The Million-Dollar Map looks very similar to a stalker wall. You know that collage of pictures, 3x5 cards, and newspaper articles that you see in police dramas. When they find the serial killer or other predator, they usually find one of these totally obsessive walls with strings, maps, articles, and pictures telling the story of who the stalker is targeting and why. Isn't it also crazy that the stalker wall in the predator's basement usually matches the one the FBI agent has in their office from tracking the criminal predator?

I have always been fascinated with putting together big, bold systems on walls that help businesses skyrocket in success. These stalker walls led me to develop my Million-Dollar Map nearly twenty years ago. I use this map to coach fledgling businesses when to make big moves, when to expect growth, when to add the next employee, and when to track the revenues of the business in those life cycles.

The map consists of three elements on a wall divided in thirds top to bottom. You will need a wall in your office that is at least twenty feet long to create the map.

These are target dimensions, and the wall surface area does not have to be exact. Every Million-Dollar Map will look unique and different. Do not get hung up in the details. Use these more as guidelines for you to get your plans and dreams out of your head.

You will place 30-inch white butcher paper on the wall. Create a row 200 inches long. Complete three of these, slightly overlapping so you end up with a white canvas on your wall approximately 90 inches (7.5 feet) tall by 220 inches (18.3 feet) wide.

AC's Million Dollar Map - Stage One (3 rows of butcher paper)

Now print out 18 months of calendars on 8.5" x 11" copy paper. Start with the next month from where you are when you start this exercise. Let us say you are starting this exercise and building your wall in August. Then you will start your calendar with September and complete it with February. Eighteen months of calendars in a row.

Place these calendars in order down the horizontal center of the butcher paper canvas. This will create an area 39" x 220" above the calendars and an area 39" x 220" below. The eighteen monthly calendars are the next 18 months in the life cycle of your business and your million-dollar path.

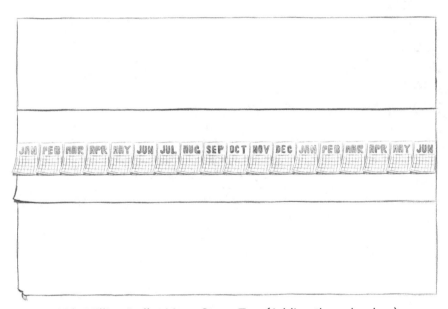

AC's Million Dollar Map - Stage Two (Adding the calendars)

Above the calendars, you will construct a line graph. The line graph will be for projecting and tracking gross revenues/sales. With a straight edge and a black marker, you will draw a bottom and top line across the entire width of the butcher paper. The bottom line is where you are today with your sales. The top line will be the million-dollar amortization mark. That being what your goal is to produce monthly in sales or revenues a number that will over twelve months hit one million dollars in a single year.

Now measure the halfway point between the two marks several times along the width of the paper and create a center horizontal line. Do this process again between the bottom line and the middle line as well as the top line and the middle line. Again, do the same until you end up with nine horizontal black lines along the top third of the butcher paper. Now, label these lines. Follow this format below.

$80K = One Million Dollars
$70K
$60K
$50K
$40K
$30K
$20K
$10K

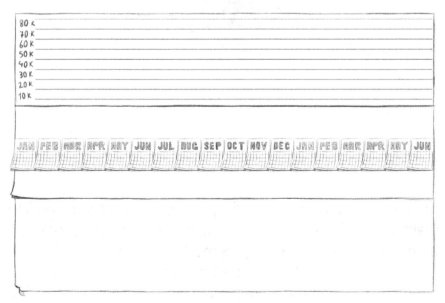

AC's Million Dollar Map - Stage Three (Building the Line Graph)

*Pat and Shielagh Clark of Precision Pro Wash
and their Million Dollar Map, 2011*

Below the calendars, you will choose your marketing niches. I like to use paper plates. Choose five paper plates, and on those, write the names of the niches you want to penetrate with your business. Niches could be residential homes or art galleries. For that matter, they could be anything based upon the product or service you are selling in your business. Pick five niches. Write them on the paper plates and staple these evenly across the bottom of your butcher paper, centered top to bottom and equally apart side to side.

Now use your imagination. Five niches divided into one million dollars is an equal $200K each. However, it is unlikely you will evenly split your revenues between the five. One or two will be more successful than the others. The goal is to represent your one million dollars of business between these five niches.

Now, grab a packet of standard 3x5 cards. You will be using these in several places along your Million Dollar Map. Around the plates, I want you to place five 3x5 cards in a circle for each niche. Grab some yarn. Any color really. It is good to go and buy about five different colors for your map. Pick a color and use a stapler. Attach a piece of yarn from each niche connecting to each 3x5 card individually. From each niche, you should have five 3x5 cards with yarn radiating out from the center of that niche. These 3x5 cards will represent the marketing channels you will use to reach those niches/prospects.

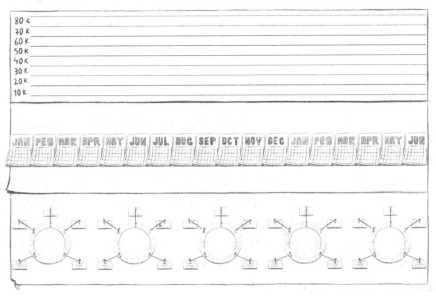

AC's Million Dollar Map - Stage Four (Adding Marketing Niches)

On each of those 3x5 cards, write a marketing channel you think will work to reach that prospect. It is totally okay if you cannot think of three. Just fill in the ones you can think of in the moment. Later, new channels will come to you, and you can fill those in later. You can change niches as easily as placing new paper plates over the old ones.

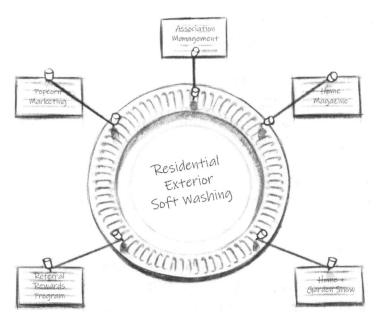

(Close Up Look of the Marketing Niches)

Next, on the single sheet calendars, let's identify every major holiday and every three-day weekend. Block out the week between Christmas and New Year's. If you are a service company, mark every Saturday and Sunday in pink highlighter. Take your off-season days (like winter), and mark those in yellow highlighter. Mark every weekday, excluding holidays and the week between Christmas and New Year's, in green highlighter. This will identify the actual working/production days of your year.

Above on the line graph, pick a color yarn for your sales projections graph. Take push pins and pick a goal for sales each month, working your way towards annualizing one million dollars. By knowing where the seasonality of your business lies, you can adjust the goals based upon the calendar, picking a monthly goal for sales and placing the pin on the timeline. Once all eighteen pins are in place, take a long piece of yarn and twist the yarn around each push pin, joining it to the next until all eighteen pins are connected in an up-and-down line graph. This is your Sales Projection line.

Each month, you will also place a push pin where your sales land and, likewise, connect the pins in a different colored yarn showing how close you got to your projection goal each month.

Pick the date you want to launch your first truck. Write on a 3x5 card "LAUNCH FIRST TRUCK," and staple it to the line graph above the calendar. Staple a piece of yarn from that card to the exact date on the calendar. Do the same with your second, third, and fourth trucks. Create 3x5 cards for hiring benchmarks (i.e., HIRE ADMIN) and pick the date, add the yarn, and staple the 3x5 card to the line graph. Examples of other milestones that can be added to the wall are "RENT SHOP" or "ADD SALESPERSON." The more milestones you place on the wall, the more DELIBERATE you will be in trying to achieve those milestones by that goal on the timeline.

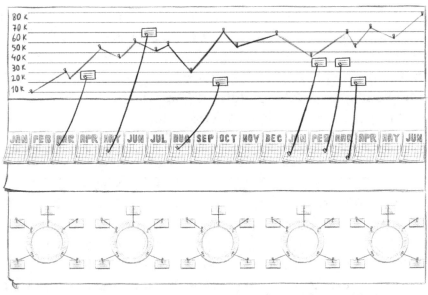

AC's Million Dollar Map - Stage Five (The Completed Map)

I hope this has given you a picture of what a Million Dollar Map could look like for your business. It is a tool I use often to coach businesses. If you desire to learn more about this tool and build your own Million Dollar Map, visit the web link below at our website.

www.ProBizGuide.com/MillionDollarMap/

KEY NUMBER TWO - EXECUTE

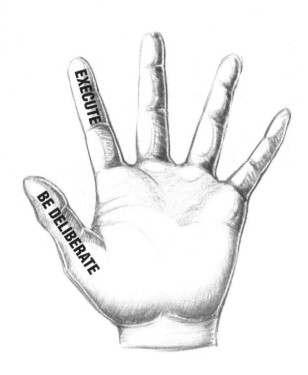

CHAPTER 6

MAKING THINGS HAPPEN

As I mentioned in the introduction, the hardest gap to close in these Five Keys to Patterning Success is the gap between BE DELIBERATE and EXECUTE. EXECUTION is where everybody gets hung up, some longer than others.

Have you ever had a friend or a relative, somebody you know, who is characterized as a dreamer? In society today, that term has been demonized. Yes, there are good dreamers and poor dreamers. Notice I did not say bad dreamers. There are only bad EXECUTERS.

That relative you have that has been characterized as a "dreamer" seems to always have a get-rich-quick scheme or a new idea for a business. Maybe an invention, a product they must improve, or a song they want to write. Maybe they say they want to write a book one day. We know the type. We get so desensitized to them we start to roll our eyes, bob our heads, and tune them out every time they want to talk about their next dream. Really, are most of their dreams bad ideas? Not likely. *Even a blind squirrel finds a nut once in a while.*

The facts are you do not take them seriously because they have what Howard Partridge calls FTI, Failure to Implement. They simply do not EXECUTE their ideas. If only that relative "dreamer" would act on one of these dreams and hit a home run only a couple of times, you would respect them completely differently. Their issue is not the dreaming part. It's in them to be DELIBERATE. The failure and issue are in the EXECUTION.

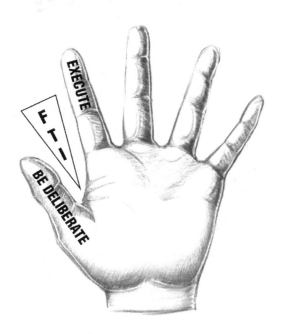

EXECUTION is also a personality trait. Robert A. Rohm, Ph. D. is the father of the modern American DISC assessment for understanding personality traits and using that understanding to develop great teams. The DISC Model of Human Behavior, in its most basic form, breaks down people into four major personality groups. D = Dominant, I = Inspiring, S = Supportive and C = Cautious. Each of these major personalities views EXECUTION differently.

The D personality type is Outgoing/Task-oriented. They view almost everything as a conquest. This type is made up of the work horse, "put your head down and pull the plow" mindset. They take risks. They make big moves. They like to win! They like results! They are comfortable with change and even crave it. This personality style represents between two and ten

Making Things Happen

percent of the population. This group usually has no issue EXECUTING. If others have FTI, this group often can have Over-Implementers Syndrome.

The I personality style is an Outgoing/People-oriented group. More about relationship than task. They are dreamers. They have big plans and have great vision. However, these are the people who talk a lot about their dreams but may not act upon their dreams. They are delegators, commonly pulling others into their plan and having others work out the details and EXECUTE.

I's never meet a stranger, always carry the conversation, and have many unfinished projects. This group usually is where your dreamer relative resides. The I personality trait represents between twenty-five to thirty percent of the population.

The S personality style is Reserved and People-oriented where your servants live. This group is less about task and more about teamwork and the relationship. They care deeply about how people will react to their dreams, moves, and EXECUTION. They crave safety and security. Think of all of the S personality words like steadiness, sacrificial, safety, and alike.

This group moves slowly because of the thought of inconveniencing others. "How will this affect my neighbor?" The trick is keeping S styles from getting caught up in the EXECUTION weeds. This personality type is the largest group in society and represents between Thirty to thirty-five percent of the population.

Finally, we have the C personality type, Reserved and Task-oriented. Described as cautious, calculated, concerned, conservative, this group is very task-oriented but will not EXECUTE until everything is correct. They are rule abiders. They count and consider every move many times before EXECUTING.

The C personality type is great at protecting money. They are engineers, accountants, scientists. Their major blind spot is over-thinking a decision. They get caught up in the weeds of in-EXECUTION by going over the details again and again until everything lines up perfectly, which it never does. This group also represents only about twenty to twenty-five of the population.

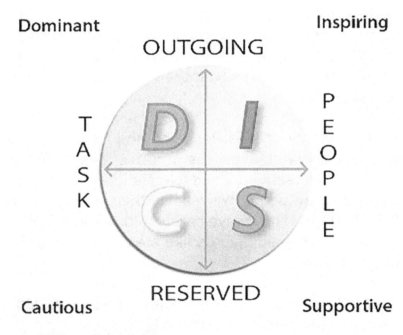

Now you have probably figured out from my short one-paragraph descriptions to which group you belong. There is a reason why you struggle with moving from

BEING DELIBERATE to EXECUTION. Most people are a combination of two or three personality types. Example: D/CI, I/SD, S/CI etc. The fact is you are built the way you are, and these are not excuses. They are facts. Facts you must deal with, but not limitations to your success. You just need to take ownership of these unique identifiers and grow past them.

The late Zig Ziglar has a quote.

> *"You are designed for accomplishment.*
> *Engineered for success. Endowed*
> *with the seeds of greatness.*
> *God doesn't make no junk."*

King David said,

> *"I am fearfully and wonderfully*
> *made." (Psalm 139:14)*

You need to remember that everyone on this earth has a purpose. Everyone has skills and talents. Everyone also has weaknesses.

God spoke to Paul and said,

> *"My grace is sufficient for you.*
> *My power is made perfect in your*
> *weaknesses." (II Corinthians 12:19)*

We all have weaknesses. We all have doubts. We all have self-limiting thoughts. There is no one alive or dead except Jesus Christ who is perfect. Everyone meets up with resistance to their life's dreams and goals. Fear is created by the evil one who plants doubt and suspicion in your mind. This is all to keep you from accomplishing the great works God has prepared in advance of your birth for you to do. (Ephesians 2:10)

EXECUTION is not a clean and easy process. EXECUTION IS NOT A CLEAN AND EASY PROCESS. Do you hear me?

Resistance and trials just might mean you are on the right path. Remember my quote,

> *"Nothing admirable is ever easily accomplished, and success rarely goes uncriticized."*

Rarely goes easy.
Rarely goes without strife.
Rarely goes without costs.
Rarely goes without loss of relationships.
Rarely goes without drama.
Rarely goes without sacrifice.
Rarely goes without a period of darkness.

If you live DELIBERATELY and EXECUTE your vision and plans, if these plans are for good and glorify God ... expect resistance!

Now as far as DISC personality styles go, around seventy percent of the world population is some combination of the S personality style, either a pure S or a combination like an IS, SI, SC, or CS. That means that the majority of us are wired to resist change and second guess ourselves. It is not your fault this seems hard. It is hard inherently for you.

I like to use the example of going to a theme park. Once you get there, you think, "Wow! I think I would like to try that roller coaster." You walk by the roller coaster a few times, sizing it up. You mention to your friends, "I think this is the day I am going to ride that coaster." You play out in your mind how you're going to prepare yourself for that coaster. What car you're going to ride in. Middle row, front, or rear. All of this is elementary until you finally get in line for the roller coaster.

Now you're in line. You were DELIBERATE. You had a plan. You even lightly EXECUTED your plan by committing to jumping in line for the coaster. Now you're winding back and forth through the line. The expected wait time is about 20 minutes. In that 20 minutes, you start to doubt your decision.

© Lawrence Rayner. This image was originally posted in Flickr:
https://flickr.com/photos/55222989@N07/5143123646

You confide with your friends that you are getting cold feet. Some affirm you, and some choose to tease you. As the line twists back and forth, you get close enough to the edge of the ride to see the coaster and hear the screams of those enjoying the ride and those who are not.

The line also winds by places you can easily jump out of line, and you consider that strongly. You get several chances to drop out of line and choose not to. Your heart starts to beat out of control. You start to sweat. A good friend puts their hand on your shoulder to console you. A questionable friend pokes at you and makes you squirm.

Finally, you reach the platform where the coaster attendant loads you onto the cars. You see a door off to the side where you have one last chance to reconsider your decision to take the ride or to exit and wait below for your friends to finish the ride. You are now at the true point of EXECUTION. Do you move forward with your plan to ride the roller coaster?

You see people who have successfully completed the coaster come into the station. Some white, pale, and distressed. Most, though exhilarated, laughing, and bouncing away, saying, "Let's ride it again! Let's ride it again!" Though all seemed to be screaming while on the roaring ride.

You take a deep breath. You move into a seat, pulling the lap bar down and securing yourself for the ride. You question yourself, "Should I cry out to the operator and ask for the bar to be released?" Your good friend grabs your hand, looks into your eyes, and smiles, assuring you they are with you. Your questionable friends laugh, tease, and say, "Last chance, scaredy pants."

The coaster car engages with the ride's chain and pulls away from the station. There is no turning back now. You have EXECUTED, and all you can do is enjoy the ride. This is the fear that goes through every entrepreneur, every time they start a new business, launch a new product, approach a new prospect.

This feeling is not really fear; it is the feeling of being alive. Once you have ridden the roller coaster a few times, you start to crave that feeling. It is called an adrenaline rush.

The coaster starts up the hill. Clank, clank, clank the chain taunts as the car is pulled up the large first hill. As you crest over the top of the hill you can see for what seems for miles as you realize how high up you are. The car pauses for just a moment as momentum dogged by gravity pulls the chain of cars over the edge of the hill and plummets you down towards the ground headed for your first curve.

Your stomach drops as the car hurls up and down through highs and lows much like your business and personal life. You are jerked right and left as you encounter curves and spirals that disorient you and make you regret deciding to take the ride.

You gasp for air from fear of being thrown from the fury of the force of the abrupt changes. You scream from the surprise and elation of the steep fast falls and turns. You suddenly realize the ride will not kill you. It will grow you. You start to relish the decision and crave the next unexpected curve.

The ride comes to an end. The car pulls into the station, and the ride operator releases the bar. You stand up a little afraid. Slightly disoriented. Somewhere between traumatized and exhilarated. You look at your friend, and they smile back at you. You both begin to laugh and say, "Let's ride it again; let's ride it again."

You realize it was all about you getting out of your comfort zone and allowing growth to happen. The roller coaster freed you from your self-limiting beliefs.

Knowing all of this now, let's look at the definitions surrounding EXECUTE.

EXECUTE
Carry out or put into effect.

EXECUTION
Putting into effect a plan, order, or course of action.

EXECUTED
To carry out effectively.

I want you to merge all three of these uses or definitions together to describe your EXECUTION process.

<u>OUR EXECUTE DEFINITION</u>
To carry out a plan, order, or course of action effectively.

The only thing standing between you having a dream and EXECUTING that dream is buying into the fear you accept into your life. Leap! Don't look back. Jump off the cliff, and build the parachute on the way down. Do not take yourself too seriously. Surround yourself with jumpers and learn how to fly.

CHAPTER 7

THE END OF THE WORLD

So ... it was the end of the world as I knew it.

I remember this as if it were yesterday. I was in the middle of a great family business turmoil. I had a selfish general manager sucking my business dry. Along with that, the economic crash of 2008 had finally hit Florida, which had been somewhat isolated, and our housing market crashed. It was the perfect storm, and I was getting rocked.

I used to witness people who watched "Daytime Dramas" Soaps, and I often heard some of the storylines that came from those trash TV shows. Shaking my head in disbelief as to the outrageousness of the content, I would wonder, "Who has that kind of drama in their lives?" Come to find out, I was about to be wrapped up in my own daytime drama storyline.

You know those times in life. The proverbial "Schmidt hit the fan" moments where everything blows up in your face. You stand back, covered in excrement, numb and in shock, with a dumbstruck look on your face. You think, "What the heck just happened?" What just happened is your chickens just came home to roost.

If you look back honestly and you take a sober accounting of all you have done in life and where you are today, you should realize even the bad stuff shapes you for the better.

If you're "really" mature and have "arrived" (LOL), you might even recognize you had it coming.

Hebrews 12:7-11 NIV *" Endure hardship as discipline; God is treating you as his children. For what children are not disciplined by their father? If you are not disciplined—and everyone undergoes discipline—then you are not legitimate, not true sons and daughters at all. Moreover, we have all had human fathers who disciplined us and we respected them for it. How much more should we submit to the Father of spirits and live! They disciplined us for a little while as they thought best; but God disciplines us for our good, in order that we may share in his holiness. No discipline seems pleasant at the time, but painful. Later on, however, it produces a harvest of righteousness and peace for those who have been trained by it."*

In 2008, the perfect storm was brewing with the financial markets being unstable and the real estate market bubble bursting, adding a tremendous strain on my business. Additionally, also on my father's investments and, as a result, our relationship. Things went horribly wrong; however, this was an instrument from God used to institute some real and significant change in my life. It is a raw and difficult story in its entirety, but much of it will go untold.

I have reconciled with my father. For nearly seven years, we did not speak. I am, after all, not the first person to have daddy issues.

3 of the 4 generations of Alfreds. Alfred CW Lockyer (1900-1966)
(L-R) AC Lockyer, AJ Lockyer (son), AL Lockyer (dad)

While all of this was happening, I had a trusted general manager that had been with me since 2002. He was an intricate part of the business and brought huge value and experience to our operation. He was a capable and calculated person.

This GM also had some financial issues in his life. As our company grew, so did his income. This GM had a package in excess of six figures, had full family health insurance, a company vehicle, expense account, and more. You know, a well taken care of team member, appreciated to the hilt.

Though this team member was well compensated, his personal financial life left him continuously in want. This continuously added stress to the business relationship. So much stress that I often questioned in my mind the value he brought to the business versus the stress of his financial instability.

Because of the difficult economic times, coupled with a greedy operations manager and family conflicts, I exited the business to cover my debts. I sold my business, and I signed a three-year non-compete. I was out of business, jobless, and broke down to my last $250. I was living paycheck to paycheck on a $250K/year package, and that gravy train was now GONE. I felt I had absolutely no way to create income.

Soon my cars would be repossessed. My boats repossessed. My RV repossessed. My home would go into foreclosure. My kid's private "Christian" school would turn us out. Everything I had worked so hard to build or create would evaporate before my eyes. I felt broken and abandoned, a complete failure.

It was a dark time for me. However, because I had surrounded myself with quality, loyal, and Christian friends, I had great counsel around me. This great counsel was not by mistake. First, God was with me. He never left my side. Secondly, my wife Karen was a HUGE support and loved me through all of this.

My best friends Roy Reid, Dan Holland, and Kevin Hipes loved up on me and talked me through the aftermath. They encouraged me, and they gave me inspiration and ideas to see me through until my next thing.

This was not by accident or because of circumstance. I picked these men to be in my life. This was a DELIBERATE action that was EXECUTED because of years of discipleship and instruction in Christian living. You are in essence, the sum of the people you surround yourself with. I knew and believed that. I chose my associations closely. I EXECUTED the life-long teachings and examples that had been set before me since I was a young boy.

Now to the real, real, real story behind the story. I know you are struggling right now about how the story of this turmoil in my life relates to EXECUTION. (Unless you are wondering if I am about to be EXECUTED myself.) Trust me, we all have these moments in our lives. You need to know how to move on from them. You need to know how to form that DELIBERATE plan and then EXECUTE that plan. We all find ourselves starting over.

I realized that between the blow-up in my family and the final selling of my business to cover my debts, the process took about ten months. For a while, I fought the inevitable.

Finally, while on a fortieth anniversary trip for my in-laws to Ruidoso, New Mexico, I had some time to sit and process all that had gone on in the last year. The condo we were staying at as a family was on Camelot Mountain, and all the back decks faced Sierra Blanco a 5,200-foot snowcapped mountain.

The mountains of Lincoln County, New Mexico, are a stop-over for about 13 species of hummingbirds as they migrate from their winter home in Mexico and travel north to their nesting grounds for the summer. This particular July, there was an explosion of hummingbirds like never seen before in the region. It was wonderous. Just the kind of distraction I needed at that moment.

I sat every day on the back deck watching the hummingbird feeders attract hummers. There were hummer wars over the feeders. The air was full of hummingbirds almost as thick as mosquitos in a humid Florida swamp.

I took out my phone (this was the year 2010 and yes, we had smartphones by then), and began to look up the types of hummingbirds. The regions they frequented. Which ones migrated through New Mexico. Which took residency in New Mexico. Their colors, shapes, behaviors. In a few short days, I was a walking, spouting encyclopedia on hummingbirds. I had found something to occupy my mind and push out the self-pity I was gripped by. (This is an important point I just made.)

If you follow me and my businesses, you may know my holding company logo has a hummingbird in it. You now know the significance of that small bird in my life. If you want to know another motivation for me using that smallest of birds as my personal brand, please read the story of the "Hummingbird and the Forest Fire" at the end of this book.

When my wife and I returned home after the trip, we settled down into our own bed for a good night's sleep. You know how it is when you travel; you cannot wait to get home to your bed to get a good night's sleep. However, that night I was restless. I could not sleep. I had thoughts going back and forth, weighing outcomes, considering options. The thoughts of the drama that had gripped my life loomed heavy on my mind. I eventually fell asleep.

When I awoke the next morning, I rolled over to kiss my bride and tell her good morning. I said to her, "Honey, I barely slept last night. I was up and down all night." Karen looked back at me and said she was as well. (I am guessing the few times I did sleep were the times she was awake.) Karen looked at me and asked me what kept me from sleeping.

I looked deep into her eyes and replied. "I just feel like we are fighting God. All of this feels unnatural. I think God is allowing us to go through this trial to drive us to another place." My helpmate then looked back at me and said she also had come to that same conclusion overnight, and we agreed the Holy Spirit was speaking to us.

That morning, I called my attorneys and had them prepare the necessary paperwork for the transfer of my company to my father, and I moved on to whatever God had for me next.

Literally, I EXECUTED the will of God at that moment. I decided to move on. I recognized the unnatural course I was on, and I decided to take immediate action. Did it hurt? Yes. Was I afraid? Yes. However, I knew it was unhealthy for me and my wife to remain in this station of our life, and it was time to be faithful and look to God for the answers.

In my mind's eye, the next two months seem like two years. Time moved so slowly as our life began to unravel. This was God stripping away the things that so easily entangled us from living our best life. (Hebrews 12:1)

One night, my buddy Roy set up a time to come by my house and check on me. He knew I was in a rut and was discouraged, and he wanted to do whatever he could to encourage me and help me get to my next stage in life. Roy has always been a huge cheerleader for me and many others. He has influence in the Central Florida community because he cares deeply about others and strives to connect people bettering their lives and the community.

Roy was sitting in my home office, working with me through the fabric of my life. Certainly, the recent challenges but also affirming my talents, opportunities, and blessings that I could build upon to create my next thing.

I had an industry event I was scheduled to speak at in September that had been scheduled before the recent events. Roy thought that was a perfect opportunity for me to launch something new. Roy helped me realize that I had so very much going for me.

For one, I had built and run two cleaning companies that grossed millions of dollars a year. I had built a business that was turnkey and allowed me to take off 150 days a year to pursue my dream of being a professional tournament fisherman. I had fished the Redfish Tour and, in my rookie season, won a National Championship. I was a good speaker and a better teacher. I was a third-generation service business entrepreneur. He pointed out I had the perfect resume and pedigree to hang out my shingle and sell my services as a business consultant. He was right on.

You know what I did after that meeting with Roy? I was DELIBERATE. I came up with a personal brand. **AC Lockyer, The Professional Business Guide**. I created a logo. I put together a small website. I created a Facebook page. I printed 100 business cards, and I went to that industry event, reinvented and confident.

AC speaking at his first cleaning convention in 2010

I spoke to the audience and spoke about my businesses that had grossed over $20,000,000 and cleaned more than 25,000 roofs, the business and marketing systems

I created to run those companies, and how making those businesses allowed me to be a husband, father, serve at church, coach my kids' teams, and even win a national championship. Then I gave my pitch. "If you want me to guide you through the wilderness of business to catch more customers, meet me off the stage, and I will be happy to give you a card and tell you how I can help."

That day changed my life for the better forever. Everything you see today came from me making a simple, DELIBERATE plan and EXECUTING it in a small measurable way. One keynote speech and 100 business cards.

CHAPTER 8

SIMPLE STEPS FORWARD

EXECUTION is scary to many, daunting to some, and unsettling for the overthinkers. When it is time to EXECUTE the plan, you have been dreaming of, things get real very quick. In my best southern United States colloquial expression, *it is time to crap or get off the pot!*

In the previous chapter, I gave you some of my background story. It gave you a glimpse into a season of drama and uncertainty in my life. You certainly realize by now drama and uncertainty are not socio-economic, gender-biased, color-bigoted, or educational prejudiced. Everyone has drama and uncertainty in their lives. To use these as an excuse is lunacy.

With a few simple steps forward, I worked myself through this season of drama and uncertainty as can you. Every good work starts with a few simple steps forward. I want to teach you my simple steps system so that you can pattern success in your own life. So here is my system...

PICK THREE SIMPLE THINGS YOU CAN EXECUTE THIS WEEK.

What? Okay, AC, you're killing me here. Is that the system?

Yes, it is. It is that simple. I did call this chapter "Simple Steps Forward," didn't I? You have to admit we all make this EXECUTION thing WAY BIGGER than we need to. We all make a *"mountain out of a mole hill."* Literally, we overthink the EXECUTE stage, and that grips us in FTI (failure to implement).

Think of it this way ... If you started out each week with three small goals, in a year, you would set 156 goals. If you were a "D" achiever, you would accomplish 109 goals this year. In many people's minds, you would be an over-achiever.

Gary W. Keller is the President of Keller Williams Real Estate and is the best-selling author of the book The One Thing. In his book, Gary argues, "What is the one thing that, if you focused on that solely, would make everything else either easier or unnecessary?" I discovered this book more than six years after my season of drama and uncertainty; however, the premise still holds true. I have embraced Gary's theology on The One Thing concept but also sprinkled some of my own lifelong experience, decorating his theology tree with a few of my own ornaments.

Let's remember back to the stage where I transitioned from the season of drama and uncertainty to the season of prosperity. I knew I needed to reinvent myself. I knew I needed to create an income. I knew I needed to move forward from the last stage of my life that was depressing and filled my mind with self-doubt. It was time to come up with a DELIBERATE plan and EXECUTE the plan.

Looking back, there were three small goals I made that created every opportunity I have experienced from that point forward.

1. Go to the cleaning convention as AC Lockyer, The Professional Business Guide.
2. Keynote the cleaning convention as AC Lockyer, The Professional Business Guide.
3. Pass out 100 business cards at the cleaning convention as AC Lockyer, The Professional Business Guide.

That is all I focused on for that week—getting to the convention and making those three things happen. Now, I do admit there were smaller actions that needed to be taken to accomplish these goals. This is called a Goal Setting Tree. This is where Gary Keller's theology will set in as well.

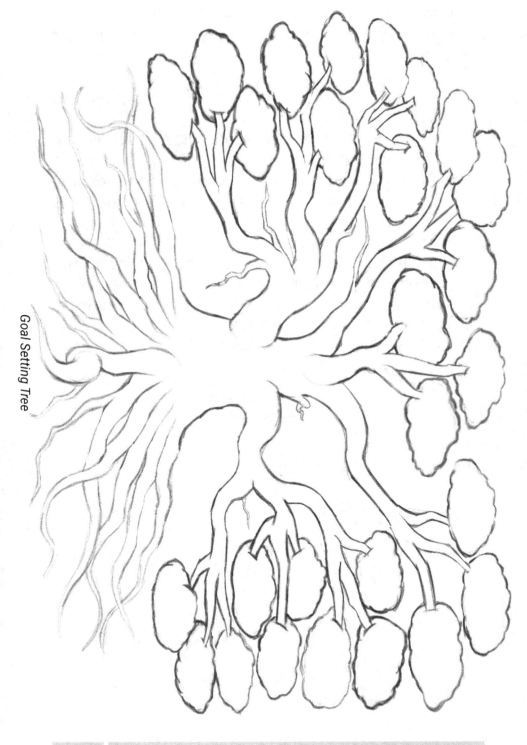

Simple Steps Forward

Imagine a beautiful oak tree. Complex and beautiful, above the ground, it has a thick robust trunk, branches, and hundreds of thousands of thick green leaves. This visual is familiar to us because the concept of a family tree is similar to a Goal Setting Tree.

It is foundationally different because at the base of the trunk of a family tree, you place your family name, and then up through the branches, you show your family associations, great grandparents, grandparents, parents, uncles and aunts, brothers, and sisters. Who married whom and whose kids belong to whom. Instead of this association, I want you to place at the base or trunk of the tree your One Thing. For me, it was to become AC Lockyer, The Professional Business Guide.

Below the surface, you have the roots of the oak tree. Literally, an inverted tree, so to speak. Here you can brainstorm and place all of the previous talents, education, opportunities, challenges, and experiences that have made you who you are today, up and until this One Thing moment. These previous positives and negatives are what has led you to this point, and they deserve to be noted.

After the trunk of the tree, there are three intersections of primary branches. These are the three simple goals you need to EXECUTE to accomplish your One Thing (at least this week). From these primary branches, there is secondary growth, or smaller branches, that emanate out and away from the primary branches. These are the actions you will need to take to accomplish your three small goals or simple steps.

Even simple steps have many actions that, once combined, accomplish the step. As you gaze at an oak tree in nature, you see the structure also includes stems. Stems are the last stage of growth before the leaf of the tree. So in order, you see this pattern on a mighty oak.

Roots – Your previous talents, education, opportunities, challenges, and experiences that have made you who you are today.

Trunk – The One Thing that will make everything else either easier or unnecessary.

Primary Branches – The three simple steps forward you need to EXECUTE to accomplish your One Thing.

Secondary Branches – The three smaller steps you will need to EXECUTE to accomplish the three simple steps forward.

Stems – The actions or deliverables that need to be EXECUTED that, in and of themselves, are mundane or meaningless.

Leaves – The resources or materials you will need.

Let me take one of my goals from the previous chapter to help you see how I planned out the EXECUTION of my DELIBERATE goal in this Goal Setting Tree format.

Roots – I was a Bible major in college. I love to share my knowledge and help others. I have a horticulture degree. I love the outdoors. I won the Redfish Tour National Championship as a professional fisherman. I am a third-generation service business owner.

Trunk – I want to become AC Lockyer, The Professional Business Guide.

Primary Branch A – Keynote the cleaning convention.

Secondary Branch A – Write a keynote for the convention.

Stem A-1 – Pick a topic for my keynote.

Stem A-2 – Develop or create a PowerPoint slide presentation for my keynote.

Stem A-3 – Bring a visual aide for my keynote.

Leaves A – Bring the AC Croc Hat. Bring The National Championship Trophy. Make sure PowerPoint is up to date on the laptop. Bring the said laptop. Have Karen check the spelling and grammar on the presentation. Rehearse the presentation. Time the presentation to 45 minutes.

Secondary Branch B – Dress appropriately for the role.

Stem B-1 – Go by barber and get haircut four days before the event.

Stem B-2 – Wear a fishing guide motif while speaking.

Stem B-3 – Check with event organizer for possible dress code.

Leaves B – Bring Redfish Tour sublimated fishing jersey. Pack khaki long pants. Set appointment at barber. Pack a belt and appropriate shoes.

Secondary Branch C – Advertise that I am keynoting the convention.

Stem C-1 – Talk up the fact I am keynoting at the convention on the internet bulletin boards.

Stem C-2 – Talk up the fact I am keynoting at the convention on social media.

Stem C-3 – Engage friends in the industry to rally other industry contractors to come to the cleaning convention.

Leaves C – Write a short script to share on bulletin boards. Pick some pictures to add to bulletin boards and social media post. Design an ad graphic for bulletin boards and social media. Set aside half a day to personally call and invite friends in the industry to the convention.

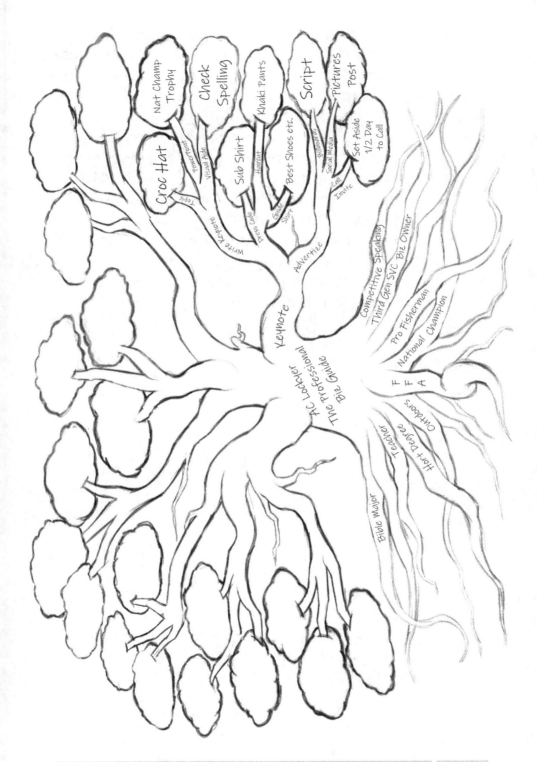

This is an exercise that will help you be DELIBERATE and prepared to EXECUTE for success every time. It starts with three simple steps forward. It is simple for a reason. You need to feel the exhilaration of the success of EXECUTION so you will begin to crave forward momentum. Big steps and huge plans are great for dreaming; however, you need to boil your plans down to easy, unintimidating steps where you don't get caught up in the weeds. Regular EXECUTION is like exercise. Once you start doing anything—even small, seemingly unimportant steps forward—you will develop a routine that will become a habit. You only need to understand this. You cannot move on in the Keys to Patterning Success in your life unless you learn to and develop the discipline of EXECUTION.

KEY NUMBER THREE - ANALYZE

CHAPTER 9
MEASURE TO MAXIMIZE

I could stop this book right here with the be DELIBERATE and EXECUTE principles. So many of you need just to get off the blocks in your life and run the race. However, true success does not lay in the EXECUTION but rather the measuring of the results of that EXECUTION.

ANALYZING and measuring your efforts is a forgotten and sometimes ignored artform in building a winning team, a flourishing company, or even a wonderful life. Without thoughtful recollection and study of your efforts, how do you know what is truly gaining traction in the success of your business?

There is a movement in culture today to eliminate measuring. You can see it in innocent arenas like childhood sports with participation trophies, all the way up to modern concepts in workplace team management. Tracking, measuring, and accountability have been marginalized and often demonized to save the feelings of fragile souls that do not desire to win in life.

Even the word *winning* has become a regaled hash tag #WINNING in the light of personalities like Charlie Sheen and his antics. Even Ricky Bobby, Will Farrell's character in the movie "Talladega Nights," coins the phrase, "Second place is just first-place loser" in regard to the attitude that he is obsessed with only settling for the win.

The fact is society is done with absolutes. If you are not a winner, then you are a loser. If you are not a producer, then you are a consumer. If you are not a conservative, then you are a liberal. You need to pay attention to the shifting of vernacular and the definition of words in our culture.

I have even noticed a trend in schools and testing. There is a huge debate among educators that dislike or downright disagree with standardized testing. (Now I have several educators in my family, so Thanksgiving is about to get real awkward after the publishing of this book.) I do not understand the entire argument surrounding Common Core, standardized testing, grading teachers, performance indicators, and alike; however, I do understand human nature.

People do not like accountability. People do not like being judged. People do not like having a grade attached to their performance. I believe wholeheartedly in benchmarks. I believe in standards. I believe in rankings. I know it is tough and uncomfortable, but human beings only grow through adversity.

AC's first Softwash Truck and Karen, 1992

If a teacher is uncomfortable with receiving a performance grade based upon their students' achieving benchmarks set forth by the department of education, then maybe they should consider a career in another field. I apologize; however, in my narrow thought process, teachers are responsible for growing students' skills in the areas of math, science, English, and social studies. (Parents instill into their children a work ethic, manners, faith, and social responsibility.)

If a teacher is ineffective in this charge, then they should receive a grade that reflects that. If they cannot overcome that deficiency, then they should lose their job. After all, isn't the entire education system for students based upon a 10-point grading system of A–F? Then why do teachers dislike being graded themselves? Why do schools dislike being graded? Is this not hypocritical?

For a short time (about two years), I was a JV football head coach. One of my weekly responsibilities was to watch the game footage from the week before and measure my team's efforts. Yes, I understand this was not varsity football it was junior varsity. My main responsibilities as a JV football coach were to:

1. Recruit players into the school's football program.
2. Teach those players the game and our varsity football coaches' system/theology.
3. Identify and develop the talents and skills of the players individually.

Notice that in these three responsibilities, I did not mention "win games" or "have fun." Winning games or having fun were not my goals as a JV football coach. Now did we win games? Ya, buddy! Did we have fun? Lots of it. In fact, during my short tenure as JV football coach, I helped grow our JV football team to over 50 players, which helped the school's entire football program reach nearly 85 players.

Because of this, our varsity football coach had an emerging pool of developed, talented players to draw from and promote up to varsity as needed. These players knew his playbook, his defense, and the entire system under which he ran his program. Yes, our JV football team won over half of our games.

Our football culture at our school grew, and these kids had fun. Did any of my players get a scholarship to play college ball? Did any make the pros? Not, one did. However, the boys in our program grew as individuals on and off the field. They had a better physical presence, had a better countenance, received better grades in their classes, and developed a strong work ethic.

There would be no way to accomplish this without developing a game, teaching them how to play it, coaching and developing them as players, and assigning points and stats to a scoreboard. You do not grow what you do not measure.

Even when I fished the Redfish Tour back in the mid-2000s, I was certainly the only angler on tour that kept Microsoft Excel spreadsheets on their fishing. Literally, I ANALYZED everything and threw it into spreadsheets to look for patterns to exploit. I had a regular routine before every tournament.

It was my rookie season, so most every tour stop I was fishing, I was unfamiliar with. Back in the day, we did not have Facebook or really any social media. We did have bulletin boards/chat rooms on the internet. These were communities where people could discuss their passions.

One passion that had many chat rooms was fishing. Especially in-shore fishing. People would chronicle their fishing trips, post pictures of their catch, and discuss the lures and tackle they used.

What everyone did not realize was that when you posted a digital picture on the web, that digital picture included code in the image of where and when that picture was taken. Literally, the GPS coordinates and exact time and date of where and when you caught that fish. I would research the tournament location in these chat rooms and download all of the pictures of redfish into a folder on my computer.

Google Maps had just come out, and one of the functions on Google Maps was the ability to upload pictures for others to enjoy. For example, if you're sightseeing in New Orleans, and you are taking pictures on Bourbon Street, and you wanted to share one of your pictures of Bourbon Street with the Google Maps community, you could upload it. Google Maps would geotag it to the exact location where you took that picture for all to see. Great for sightseeing and sharing. Not so great if you are trying to keep your secret fishing spot a secret.

I would then dump all of these redfish photos into Google Maps, and instantly, Google Maps would start organizing them onto the map by location, showing exactly where all of those fish were caught. I now had a satellite map and fish location to go and ANALYZE. Along with that, the time and date of when each fish was caught.

Now I could also go back on the tide charts and solunar table to see the tide and feeding time for each spot's best catches. All to zero in when exactly I needed to be in each spot. Finally, I would throw all of this data into a spreadsheet, ANALYZE, and sort those locations by distance from the tournament launch and tide position to create a fishing schedule. This process was deadly accurate. As you know, my tournament partner Thresher Klier and I won the Redfish Tour National Championship that year.

Knowing all of this, let's now look at the definitions surrounding ANALYZE.

ANALYZE
Examine methodically and in detail the constitution or structure of (something, especially information), typically for purposes of explanation and interpretation.

ANALYZING
To discover or reveal something usually through detailed examination.

ANALYSIS
The process of breaking a complex topic or substance into smaller parts in order to gain a better understanding of it.

I want you to merge all three of these uses or definitions together to describe your ANALYZATION process.

OUR ANALYZE DEFINITION
The process of breaking down numbers or a topic into smaller parts to reveal information that will guide you to make better-informed decisions.

The process of ANALYZATION must be mastered before you can take advantage of the fourth key, which is REPLICATION. You also cannot move forward from EXECUTION without the peace of mind that your process is working. Without running the numbers to see if, in fact, you are having real success, you cannot witness the success. Real success is only defined by forward momentum. If you are not winning, you will need to ANALYZE that and see what DELIBERATE adjustments you will need to make to your plan before moving forward.

CHAPTER 10

ANALYZE YOUR SEASONAL CURVE

As you know from reading this book, I owned a 4.8 million dollar a year soft wash cleaning company by the time I was thirty years old. It was very cool and challenging. The company grew from around eighty thousand dollars a year to $4.8 million in just six short years. So, you know we did not have a single down year in that six-year run. It was mathematically impossible. What you may not know is that even among that incredible double-digit growth year after year I felt incredibly out of touch and inadequate. It was like a baker baking the perfect cake the first time ever baking a cake and then stressing out worrying if they could replicate that effort over and over.

I had great success from two gigantic moves. First, I asked my father to come into the business with me because I was inexperienced and overwhelmed. Second, I had a strong work ethic and honestly did not let up on forward momentum, which was awesome but unsustainable. Success was coming, but it was not easy. In fact, the only indicator we watched for success was how much money we were depositing from month to month. That, my friend, is a recipe for disaster.

I remember one summer after our spring rush, things started slowing down, as they do every summer. I began to feel uneasy. I started to wake in the mornings with a pit in my stomach and dreaded going into work. My team also was worried.

We all knew we were way up in sales over the previous year but did not know what to expect during the slow season. It was unsettling and eroded the confidence of my team and my ability to lead effectively. Something had to be done.

In an effort to get my hands around this slow-down, I compiled a spreadsheet of our monthly numbers for that current year. Then I layered in the previous year's numbers behind them. I saw a pattern. Then to emphasize that pattern I created a line graph on the spreadsheet to create a visual representation of the ebb and flow of the seasonality pattern I was seeing in the numbers. I began to see some light.

I dug deeper into our accounting software as well as our banking records going back five years, and I added monthly deposits alongside sales numbers and production totals. It was clear now; we had a pronounced seasonal curve to our business. As I scrubbed the numbers, making them more and more accurate. I further debunked these numbers against our accounting software and bank deposits.

AC's Softwash Business Mallard Systems, 1998

I started to get a clear picture of exactly where my company was in relation to the pronounced seasonal curve and how we grew the company year over year for the same months. (Example: August 1997 versus August 1998 versus August 1999) What I found was that we were about to have our best August ever in business. Albeit it was a down month compared to the trends coming out of May, June, and July, this was about to be a record August.

Suddenly I felt energized, excited, victorious. I now knew that August SUCKS, and as far as sucky Augusts go, we were having the best possible sucky August we could have. We were up. We were poised to have a record September. We were sowing the seeds to have an awesome fall.

In fact, when you layer in the percent of growth month over month from May, June, July, and August, I could apply that average percent of growth to the rest of the year and project the revenues for September, October, November, and December. Suddenly, we were killing it. The narrative completely changed.

I took that new spreadsheet and printed thirty copies of it. I posted it on every wall in the facility, at every desk, and even attached it to a company-wide email. I called a sales meeting and discussed strategies to capitalize on the best year ever in the history of the business.

I talked about concepts like the Calm Before the Storm. I had my authority back, I had a vision to share, and I got rid of the pit that was inside my stomach. Measuring was not a curse; it was a path to freedom. From that time forward, ANALYZING numbers and measuring efforts has become my primary management tool for success in my companies.

Tools and SYSTEMS can be very visual. Long before my obsession with 50" LED TV screens came to exist, I was creating big, visual, audacious tracking systems on the walls of my offices. I learned this from my father who was a second-generation service business owner.

I remember in the mid-1980s, my father had an appliance delivery and installation company. Do you remember the song Money for Nothing by Dire Straits? The chorus went like this:

We have to install microwave ovens,
Custom kitchen delivery.
We've got to move these refrigerators,
We've got to move these color TVs.

I thought somebody was stalking me and my family. It was crazy and weird that a rock-n-roll song would have a chorus about our family business, but that is exactly what my father did for a living when that song came out.

The big difference was he had a fleet of ten trucks rocking that tune six days a week. Those ten trucks had six to eight tickets they had to run a day, and scheduling/dispatching those trucks was a nightmare if you did not have a great system in place. There were no computers in those days. Not really. No software to do this task. Certainly not an app. Everything was analog and hands-on.

My father remodeled a house in a commercial area to serve as the shop for this business. He enclosed the two-car garage and turned it into a dispatch office. Two of the walls in the dispatch office were completely open and led to a corner in the middle. My father glued cork onto those walls making them huge cork boards.

Analyze Your Seasonal Curve

He divided those two walls into "current week" and "next week." Sectioned the walls into Monday–Saturday columns across the top and Truck 01–Truck 10 down the sides as rows. Below these boards was a continuous countertop with plenty of workspace.

Smack in the middle of the dispatch room was an island much like you would have in a kitchen. That was the workspace for the dispatcher. The room had a phone system, two-way radio system, and bins for incoming work orders that would feed onto the cork boards by day of the week and by truck. It was all color-coordinated in company colors and had a purposeful look to it. The room was very impressive, and every visitor to my father's company was awed by the detail.

These were the types of systems I was exposed to when I was growing up. Big and visual, they helped steer companies and create culture. These big, physical, tangible wall systems had an effect on the professionalism of the company and called everyone higher.

As I encountered more obstacles in the businesses I would start and grow, I was met with similar challenges. Some challenges could be addressed by running some numbers, looking at indicators, ANALYZING the records, and emailing a memo to the team. Others required constant ANALYZATION and tangible visual accountability so that the team could rally around these numbers ... much like a scoreboard.

I soon realized that my employees/teammates were ANALYZING the company's position and ability to score as much as I was. They were just more silent about it. At least to me. The truth was there is always back-channel talk that happens in your company, and life for that matter.

The people around you are ANALYZING your performance to see if they want to follow you as a leader or not. Your ability to stay ahead of them by getting them the data they need to do their jobs and feel secure in their positions is paramount. These wall systems can be a way to equip and calm the team, poising them for winning performance.

Mallard Systems Dispatch Board, 1998

At my soft washing company Mallard Systems, I created a big visual dispatching experience. We also added weekly and monthly sales boards. Alongside that, we created our leads and pinks wall chains that are a part of our current SoftServ Business System. Even the crews out doing the soft wash cleanings had a leader board in the warehouse that we called The Wall of Fame/Wall of Shame. Every place I had an open wall in my facilities, I purposed that wall and tracked the efforts of the company. That created a driven and winning culture.

In business and in life, you need to slow down and ANALYZE where you are and adjust where you are going. Profit and loss statements, balance sheets, and financial statements only tell a small part of your company story and are largely reactional and viewed monthly after the results. Daily and up-to-the-minute ANALYZATION is key for real-time adjustments to win the overall daily game of business.

CHAPTER 11

MVPS SCOREBOARDS AND STATS

Let's stop a minute and be honest. There is really no such thing as a right or wrong decision. For me, there are only next best decisions. This is a concept that is lost on most of the world's population.

If you remember the D.I.S.C. model for human behavior, you have four different groups of people "basically." D's, I's, S's, and C's. Each one of these groups has natural predispositions to being Outgoing or Reserved, Task-oriented or People-oriented. That makeup leads these four major groups to being either quick decision-makers or, in the other extreme, those who get caught up in the decision-making weeds.

Each group needs various amounts of input or information to make a decision. For the people-oriented groups (I's and S's), they need input from their friends or community to make a decision. For the task-oriented group (D's or C's), they need only to have facts and goals to guide them to a decision.

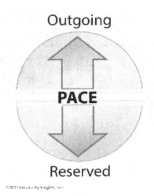

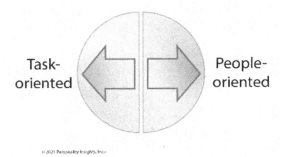

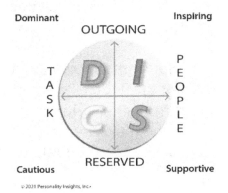

Outgoing and Reserved, Pace + Task-Oriented,
and People-Oriented COMPASS photos

Then if you look at the reserved groups (C's and S's), they are slow to make decisions because they are either very conservative or they are very relational. In study and observation, the I's, S's, and C's move more slowly and need more information/facts in the decision-making process.

The D's stand almost completely alone in being quick and risk comfortable with making fast and decisive decisions. Though this seems like a perceived strength in the D personality style (and yes, it can be), it also can create blind spots for leaders in their businesses if they are a high D personality style. One example of this is making decisions based upon expedience and neglecting to consider relationship. This can be a fatal flaw for the D personality style.

My life has been a study and adjustments of how I work. How I perform. What drives me? Where do my successes come from? How can I REPLICATE those successes? It took me many years to become comfortable with who I am and, more importantly, who I am not. This is a process of self-awareness that all individuals should explore.

For my success, I realized I need quick, timely data to make a decision because I am impatient. I need data on hand that is ever-evolving. I need that data most importantly so I can bring my team alongside me during the decision-making process and give them the information and security their personality styles crave.

I was at a graduation commencement back in 2017, and the commencement keynote speaker was delivering a talk on leadership in the workplace. He gave a quote that has burned into my mind since then and guided me in being a bold leader for my tribe.

> *"Leadership is the art of disappointing your people at a rate that they can tolerate."*
> **John Ortberg**

The key here is these three facts:

1. Change is not comfortable, and leading people through change, which is constant, will disappoint your tribe.
2. The rate of tolerance can be greatly expanded the more information and communication you bring to your tribe.
3. They are only your people if they have a relationship with you. Stop to love your people.

Point one I have no control over. People are fearfully and wonderfully made in the image of the almighty God; however, they are broken and fallen. I have no responsibility or control over their comfort.

I can, however, have much control over the flow and availability of information and the communication of that information to my tribe. Here is where you need to focus when dealing as a D with the three other major personality groups.

What I have discovered is, as a D, the tools I need in place to make sure I don't drop the ball or move erratically in my life can be wonderful tools of communication when shared appropriately with my team. Over the years, I have honed these systems into a plan I call my MVPs, Scoreboards, and Stats Program. Here is how this program works.

MVPs

One of my mentors, Howard Partridge of Phenomenal Products, has what he calls his MVPs. That is your Mission Statement, Vision Statement, and Purpose Statement. These are three short documents, usually only a paragraph long. They describe what your company does, where you want to go, and who you want to serve. They can be more robust or very simple. The key here is to make sure you have MVPs in your business so that your team knows what the game is we are playing.

A company without MVPs becomes a company that is run and ruled by an owner that imposes his will over his subjects. Everything, day-to-day, comes down to what the boss wants, what the boss said, and the accountability of the boss. Without MVPs, you are relegated to becoming a dictator.

If you have MVPs in your business and your team was invited to the workshop to create the MVPs, then the operations and accountability of the business swing away from rule by dictatorship to adherence to the principles of the document. This is not a new concept. Have you ever heard of the U.S. Constitution?

Now the MVP's only work if you make them the center of your company. We post them everywhere. On the company communication bulletin board. We post them at team members' desks. We recite them at company meetings. We keep these MVPs ever mindful in our companies. It keeps the team centered on what it is we are trying to accomplish.

Here are examples of one of my companies' MVPs.

Mission

To leave a lasting legacy, nurturing soft washing businesses, and fostering opportunities in faith, family, hope, and community.

Vision

To see one-thousand soft washing businesses thriving under our business model worldwide by the year 2040.

Purpose

Put to work our God-given opportunities and talents so we can one day hear, "Well done, good and faithful servant." (Matthew 25:14-30)

By bringing these MVPs to the forefront of the business, we on the team know what our goals are, what the standard is, and what is at stake. You cannot ANALYZE your position without having a heading. You cannot navigate without knowing what, in fact, is True North. Your company MVPs will become your True North.

Our Mission

To leave a lasting legacy.
Nurturing soft washing businesses
and fostering opportunities in
FAITH, FAMILY, HOPE
and COMMUNITY.

Our Vision

SoftWash Systems vision is to see
ONE THOUSAND soft washing
businesses world wide, thriving
under our business model
by the year 2040.

OUR PURPOSE

SoftWash Systems vision is to see
ONE THOUSAND soft washing businesses
worldwide, thriving under our business model
by the year 2040.

AC's company Softwash Systems and their MVP's

SCOREBOARDS

You cannot assemble a team and ask them to play a game without structure in the way of rules, penalties, rewards, and how to achieve victory. In my mind, you simply cannot play a game without scoreboards. Scoreboards in sports not only keep score but also show what down it is, the ball position, what quarter of play the game is in, and most of all, if we are winning or losing. Your team will be lost and will not understand your decisions if they do not have a known position in the game of business.

In the early 2000s, I used dry erase boards and other very visual systems on walls to show where we stood in the game of business. They were big and audacious; it was easy for a team member to walk by and, at a glance, see what the score was and how they stacked up against their other teammates.

Purple Rhino SoftWash in the United Kingdom and their sales chains wall (pictured Ella Heales)

I had some of the dry erase boards made up by my sign provider. These were weekly sales boards, monthly sales boards, year-to-date sales by month, and others. I even had a twenty-foot by eight-foot, magnetic dry erase board in our service truck dispatching room with all twelve of our truck's schedules out two weeks.

In the sales room, I had anchored placards to the wall with the salesperson's names, picture, and territory maps, as well as two chains hanging underneath with binder clips attached. One for incoming leads and one for the NCR pink copies of completed quotes. It became a living bar graph as incoming leads were attached to the chains and the corresponding quote was hung beside the lead.

Before there were digital CRMs and Google Sheets, I used every wall in my business to show and promote effort, create accountability, keep stats, and most importantly, show the score.

The little secret was I did not build this for my team … I built it for me to cover my inadequacies and give me visual structure to manage my ever-growing business. The beauty of it was, when I did this in such a bold and visual way, the entire team rallied behind it, and these wall systems ran my business for me. My entire team participated in the ANALYZATION process and adjusted on the fly quicker than I could even verbally coach them.

Today, I have an absolute fetish for 50" LED TV screens. If you visit my companies, you will notice I have upwards of thirty throughout my facility. These scoreboards are for showing live data. What I consider live data is data in which the numbers are changing constantly throughout the day, and we want to see as they change.

Just like a scoreboard at a game. I want to know, in real-time, what adjustments I need to make now to change the outcome of the scoreboard so we can come from behind and win the game of business. Real-time ANALYZATION of your position in the game is so very important.

I have found that companies must embrace the extra work it takes to create and maintain these scoreboards in their company. Even if they do not change another single thing, they will increase sales and revenues by at least 30%. Not to mention the visual of the scoreboards elevating the look and branding of the facility these also help with company culture.

Here is a list of scoreboards I recommend you keep in any business to help rally your team and promote growth in revenues and culture.

Weekly Sales Board
Monthly Sales Board
Year-to-Date Sales versus Projections
Leads versus Sales Conversions

You can buy an inexpensive business PC and add a four-screen video card to power these scoreboards. Create your scoreboards in Google Sheets, and then display them on one of the screens through your web browser. Google sheets auto-updates/refreshes every time a change is made, either on that computer or remotely. Also, another cool thing about using Google Sheets is that you can download the Sheets app onto your phone or other devices, and as you are invited to view those scoreboards, you will be able to view them live on your phone or device anywhere in the world.

In AC's businesses, he has many 50-inch LED monitors for scoreboards. At SoftWash systems, he has in excess of 30 such scoreboards.

STATS

In the thought process of business, ANALYZATION stats may be the best first place to dig into your numbers and find the real truths about your team and company's performance. In my program of MVPs, Scoreboards, and Stats, stats represent the slower moving or slower realizing numbers you track, not on scoreboards, but rather as monthly reports, line graphs, and spreadsheets. These give you a monthly, quarterly, or yearly snapshot of where your company has been and where it is headed.

I typically track these stats and display them as 8.5" x 11" printable sheets that are displayed on our stats wall in plastic frames. I place them there for the whole team to see. I need my team to know if we are profitable. I need them to see how much we spend on items like Cost of Goods or Payroll. Whether or not we are on or off budget. These stats are a study of our intermediate and long game plans.

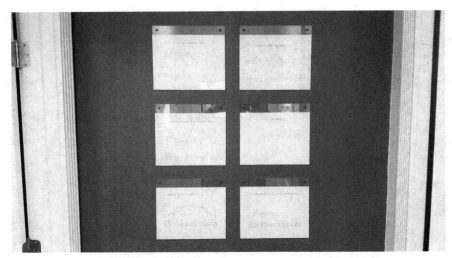

AC practices open book management with his team members. He openly shares his numbers with them.

Some of the stats I compile on at least a monthly basis are known to you. These are as simple as printing out your company's financial statement, balance sheet, monthly payables report and receivables report. These are obvious. However, some stats you may not know about, which are essential in operating a successful business, are:

Payroll vs Deposits

In many companies, especially service businesses, payroll is often the biggest expense. Payroll and related fees can comprise as much as 50% of the expenses in a service business and as low as 20% in a retail or products-driven business.

Payroll overages often eat directly into the profitability of a company. Show me a company that is unprofitable, and I will show you a company that does not have its payroll and related expenses under control. Having a spreadsheet that compares your income/deposits in relation as a percentage to the payroll spent and then graphically shown as a line graph can help you zero in on your in-budget payroll goals.

Sales vs Revenue

I know it is a shocker ... however, you may not know that what the sales team puts up on the scoreboard as a win may not ever hit the banking account as a deposit. It is a phenomenon that is present in every industry. It's not fraud. It is simply a rule of nature.

What we sell does not always result in an exacting deposit number. Stuff happens. Sales fall through. Discounts are given. Chargebacks occur. Returns come back and restocking fees are assessed. Sales boards rarely match revenue boards, and it is to be expected.

However, it is a good practice to keep a monthly spreadsheet on total sales revenue versus actual deposited revenue, including sub-categories like discounts, chargebacks, returns, and settlements. Displaying these in a frame each month-end will help your team to reduce these inconsistencies merely by bringing attention to them.

Production vs Sales

If you own a service business, another bleed you will see is the drop number between sales and production. This actually flows in this way: a product or service is sold, the job is booked and completed, or the product is shipped. Somewhere along the way, somebody dropped the ball. It could have been the shipper losing the product. Could have been the shipping desk shipping out the wrong product.

It might have been the service crew did a poor job, and a concession in the form of a discount was given. It might be a positive flow in that an upsell occurred by a non-sales employee; therefore, the new sale did not show up on the sales boards, and we are seeing more income than sales for that month. Keeping a spreadsheet with a line graph embedded can help you look for, recognize, and adjust for these important fluctuations.

Revenue vs Marketing Expense

The two biggest bleeds for a business, especially a service-based company, are number one, payroll overages and related expenses. The second may be unexpected for you. It is, however, overspending on marketing expenses. Marketing is like a drug, especially for lazy entrepreneurs.

Floundering companies not showing a profit and living on credit cards usually have an owner with an addiction of some kind. It might be drugs and alcohol. It might be sex and promiscuity. It could even be a lust for material things, and the entrepreneur is not exercising delayed gratification. More times than not, it is likely to be an addiction to marketing. In my thirty-plus years of business and mentoring/coaching business owners, I have seen the top three biggest bleeds in a business in this order.

1. Payroll overages – overtime and related expenses
2. Marketing expense – paying to make the phone ring
3. Owner's lack of discipline – not exercising delayed gratification

In a service business (and most others), you should never exceed more than 5% of your deposited revenues each month in advertising. This is a gravitational rule. Having a monthly stat will help you stay on track and not overspend on advertising.

There are so many stats and reports I have used to ANALYZE my company position and keep on True North. I even track and measure every lead that comes into my companies. How they heard about us and what form of advertising it was.

I compile that data weekly into a report for our weekly sales meetings and then grade our advertising efforts. We promote and REPLICATE good performing advertising and prune away underperforming advertising to clear up funds to throw at the marketing that is working. I will share more about this practice in the next key, REPLICATE.

ANALYZATION takes time. You need to slow down to do it. Once you get your business engine running you must take the time to tune that engine. As the leader in your business, or for that matter family, you need to be disciplined and carve out time to review and ANALYZE all your efforts, at least if you want to build a championship team.

AC's first $4500 sales in 1992. Here pictured was his desk in his bedroom while still living with his parents, after being kicked out of college.

KEY NUMBER FOUR - REPLICATE

CHAPTER 12

DEFINING INSANITY

I am sure you have heard one definition of insanity is to do the same things over and over expecting a different result. Many of us at one time or another have had some insane businesses or marketing for that matter. We seem to think that the systems and processes we have built into our lives are correct even though they are broken and not working.

We wonder, "Maybe this will work if I just focus more, put in more effort, or throw more money into _____ [fill in the blank]." We use the same marketing over and over, expecting a different result. Use the same HR practices over and over, expecting a different result. Even handle our finances the same way over and over, expecting a different result. We, thereby, are existing in an insane cycle of denial and failure, without even knowing how to work our way out of it.

REPLICATION is a double-edge sword that cuts both ways. In life, you can REPLICATE more bad decisions and actions, reaping a harvest for those actions that lead to failure and despair. Or you can identify the things that are going well for you and simply do more of that.

REPLICATE is by far the easiest and most fruitful key in my Five Keys to Pattern Success. If you have implemented great ANALYZATION processes in your business, you should be able to quickly and efficiently identify wins or losses in your everyday actions.

It sounds simplistic; however, the goal in this key is to do more of the good stuff and less of the bad. Yes, I do get the irony in that statement. It is pretty straightforward and sounds good, but so many never actually practice this simple rule of success. Do more of the good stuff.

Before you can REPLICATE the good moves you have made, thereby REPLICATING the good results, you will need to look back at the data you compiled during your daily, weekly, and monthly ANALYZATION of your business. Reviewing your data will shed light on where your wins exist.

Successful people count, record, keep spreadsheets, notes, journals, and scoreboards. If you do not develop these habits, you will not succeed in your pursuits or move onto Key Four and Five. You simply will not live the victorious life God has intended for you to live.

Now, this also will take some self-reflection of your own personal strengths and weaknesses. Often, personal success means having a healthy self-awareness of who you are, your talents and opportunities, and what you are truly capable of. Simply put, none of us is perfect. All of us have strengths and weaknesses.

Each of us needs to take a sober accounting of these strengths and weaknesses and do some personal pruning to make sure we are focused on what we are truly good at, and then REPLICATE those strengths, talents, and opportunities to our benefit and the benefit of those placed in our stewardship circle.

We are all built for a purpose. If you have an engineering mind but struggle with sales, do not waste your life trying to conform to the expectations of being a great salesperson. If you are great at sales but accounting and money are a struggle, do not seek the approval of others by hyper-focusing on all things financial in your business just to prove people wrong. Embrace who you are, and do more of what you are good at. Hire people to cover your weaknesses and clear the deck for you to soar in the areas you have been gifted.

I see so many entrepreneurs struggle with this self-realization trap. You allow others to project expectations onto you, and you waste precious time trying to be what others think you should be. This is madness and truly insanity itself.

AC and Howard Patridge

This is what I have found to be true. ANALYZE everything. Study the efforts in your company but also the strengths and talents of you and your staff. Prune away what is not working. Stop spending time and money on those useless efforts. Find out what, in fact, is working, and do more of that.

ANALYZE your personal strengths, and REPLICATE more of those.

ANALYZE your best employee, and REPLICATE more of them.

ANALYZE your winning marketing strategies, and REPLICATE more of that.

Knowing all of this, let's now look at the definitions surrounding REPLICATE.

REPLICATE
To make an exact copy of or reproduce.

REPLICATION
The action of copying or reproducing something.

REPLICATOR
A thing or process which copies or reproduces something.

I want you to merge all three of these uses or definitions together to describe your REPLICATION process.

OUR REPLICATE DEFINITION
To use a process to reproduce an action so you can copy a result over and over.

A process, an action, and a result. Let that sink in. A process, an action, and a result.

A Process – a well-placed and timely advertising campaign.

An Action – that causes the phone to ring and creates a lead.

A Result – in which a sales rep visits and closes a job.

When you identify a string like this, you need to put energy behind it and REPLICATE it.

A Process – an employee bonus for introducing new team members.

An Action – that helped us find our best machinist.

A Result – that increased production by 15%.

Now, create a SYSTEM around this win, and REPLICATE more of that.

It is a sad fact that business owners are distracted easily. I have seen so many abandon their current business strategy merely in the name of change. They seem to think that change is sexy. We will put a DELIBERATE plan to paper. EXECUTE that plan with good success. Neglect to ANALYZE that effort sufficiently. Then move on to another strategy without digging in and seeing if we can move the line graph up and to the right simply through REPLICATION.

ANALYZE and REPLICATE go hand-in-hand. After you get your business off the ground and have it humming along for a while, it is time to tune that engine. Here is a step you can add to your routine now.

Take one day each month to ANALYZE your numbers in your company. Then take two days each quarter to have a retreat away from the office to again ANALYZE your numbers as well as look specifically for wins that can be replicated. The next quarter, implement three items that are a REPLICATION of a good result you think might hold promise. Throw extra energy behind that favorable result, and see if you can magnify that result into a bigger win. If you try three new REPLICATORS per quarter, that will be twelve REPLICATORS in one year. If you have a 50% success rate, six will show results and grow your company.

If 50% of the REPLICATORS work and add 5% growth each to your company, then in one year you will have identified a way to grow your business by 30%. If you have a one-million-dollar business and you can REPLICATE this formula year after year, you will end up with a $3,712,930 business in five years.

Year 01 $1,000,000.00 x 1.30 = $1,300,000.00
Year 02 $1,300,000.00 x 1.30 = $1,690,000.00
Year 03 $1,690,000.00 x 1.30 = $2,197,000.00
Year 04 $2,197,000.00 x 1.30 = $2,856,100.00
Year 05 $2,856,100.00 x 1.30 = $3,712,930.00

This is the miracle of compound interest as well.

There are many REPLICATORS I can introduce to you and help you achieve unbelievable growth in your business. Regardless of business type or size, you can even achieve doubling your business in a single year. All you need to do is invest in and REPLICATE the wins, and prune away and discard the losses. Are you willing to test this?

CHAPTER 13

SELF-REPLICATION BY SELF-REALIZATION

Please indulge me and spend a few moments peering into my personal story and allowing me to give you an example in my own life of how I accomplished REPLICATION by self-realization.

Early on in my business career, I realized that I was a dreamer and had a bit of a problem with the doer side of that equation. I am, in my deepest crevices, a lazy individual. In fact, one of my quotable quotes is *"Necessity is not the mother of invention; laziness is."* I am sure I got a bit of a giggle from you when you read that; however, I truly believe this. I know for a fact most of my early innovation in my business life was simply because I did not want to work.

Today, I understand that work is a spiritual thing. It is an act of worship to God. A good day's work renews your soul and cleanses your spirit. You know that all-day landscaping project where you transform your front yard and stand back at the end of the day with your drink in your hand and proudly exclaim, "This is good"?

That proud exclamation "This is good" comes from our creator Himself. It is how He ended his hard days' work in the creation of the Earth. (Genesis 1:31) Remember in the beginning of this book I quoted the great Zig Ziglar and his famous line that starts with "We are designed for accomplishment"? Every single one of us is hardwired for accomplishing tasks that glorify God.

However, we are carnal in nature, and when the Earth fell because of the disobedience of Adam and Eve in the Garden, sin entered our lives and created the scenario where we fall short of what God designed us for. Laziness was born at that exact moment.

Because of the sin of laziness that was released/born in the Garden that day, we by carnal nature pursue the illustrious shortcut. Everything is a life hack today. Everything is to be automated. Even our cars must drive for us. The entire world is gripped in this "get more by doing less culture," and it is killing us.

I am no different. I am just more self-aware than most are. I have been on a 52-year journey of self-realization. I now know, with a few years of experience and some road-trodden wisdom, that there are two different formulas that exist in this world.

$$(\text{Effort} \div \text{Hours Worked}) \times \text{Optimal Minimal Output} = \text{Automation}$$
$$(\text{Effort} \times \text{Hours Worked}) \div \text{Optimal Minimal Output} = \text{REPLICATION}$$

I can literally divide the entire human race into these two groups, Automator or Replicator.

The Automator

The hallmark trait of an Automator is that Automators only want to put out X amount of effort for a desired return. Automators look at everything they can put on cruise control because they have decided that their time is worth

X, their capabilities are only X, the opportunity is only X; and in their mind, they must automate the process so that they no longer need to manage or touch that X which they have deemed automatable.

Automation is a lie and keeps leaders from REPLICATING people, process, and product. I am not a complete hater of automation. I do have a particular disdain for digital automation. Digital automation is good for small tasks like paying monthly bills, your calendar reminding you to make a follow-up call, or flashing a light on your dashboard so you do not drive your car past the capacity of its fuel cell.

However, when you fully automate your sales system, you are headed down a path to lower prices, less opportunity, and no brand/customer loyalty. Digital automation robs you of the personal touch of business. You have heard the adage that people buy from whom they know, like, and trust. Digital automation of your sales and other processes removes this important truth from your business.

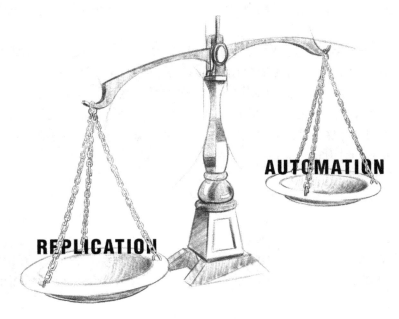

Imagine a business that flies completely on autopilot. You spend $2,000 a month on advertising. That generates 100 visits to your website. The prospect sees a lovely video of you and your family in front of your business thanking them for visiting your site, and you explain the value of using your business.

Then a form pops up where they are invited to complete a survey of their property that gives the prospect the ability to self-quote their services. Only about ten prospects actually complete the form. Then a price is given based upon the information the customer enters into the self-quoting system.

Of those, 80% (8 out of 10) like the automated price and click the submit button accepting the proposal. An email is then autogenerated to the new customer validating their selection. On that email, there is a link to go to your automated scheduling system for the customer to select their preference for booking their service. They select a date and time and await your arrival to perform the service.

Along the way, automation generates a one-week notice till their job will be completed. A 48-hour notice. A 24-hour notice. And finally, a courtesy call is made by an automated robotic voice the morning of the service call, reminding the customer of the service appointment and window of the expected arrival time.

The automated robotic voice also asks the customer to have payment ready in the form of a bank check and coaches the customer on how to prepare their property for service. Then your truck and crew show up on the job, complete the service, and return to the office with minimum contact or interaction with the customer. Wouldn't that be wonderful?

ABSOLUTELY NOT. NO WAY NO HOW.
IT IS CUSTOMER NO-SERVICE AT ITS BEST.

All an automation string like this does is create a sanitized, unfeeling experience that anyone (any competitor) can copy and reproduce. They can hire actors to do the touchy-feely videos on their website. They can automate the entire buying process, removing any chance of conflict. They can send out a crew to complete the service without ever even meeting the customer.

The entire experience is boiled down to price and convenience. There are zero true differentiators, and automation has led you down a path where the customer never bought from those they knew, liked, or trusted. They bought from an illusion. The relationship was not real. It was business automation porn.

The REPLICATOR

By contrast, the REPLICATOR sees all time as a valuable commodity that cannot be replaced or extended. Each day has only so many hours, and each hour is finite. REPLICATORS often ask themselves how to squeeze more out of their busy workday, wanting to grow their business for all of its infinite potential. REPLICATORS know the value of human interaction and build their businesses on people, not programs. REPLICATORS create jobs, promote families, send kids to college, help employees achieve their dreams, and serve customers with a personal touch.

REPLICATION as per our definition: *To use a process to reproduce an action so you can copy a result over and over.*

A REPLICATOR will look at a sales team member that is absolutely killing it and say, "Where do I find more of that person?"

An Automator will look at that sales team member and say, "It is impossible to find another person like that. I need to find a way to automate the process and eliminate the human element."

A REPLICATOR stays up late at night, sleepless, dreaming about their business and the hope and legacy it will certainly create.

An Automator will prefer to automate their business and make money while they sleep.

REPLICATORS look for the small wins and profitable results and rack their minds on how to do more of the winning formula that is already working.

I am a REPLICATOR. I had to be. There is not a secret sauce or magic formula in any of my business success. I simply have put one foot in front of the other every day of my life and EXECUTED the next best plan. When I see a plan that works, I stop and ANALYZE why it worked. Then I put together a plan to do more of that wonderful result, REPLICATING it over and over.

This became very evident in the late 1990s when the dot-com boom was happening, and unemployment in the State of Florida had reached an all-time low. There was absolutely no one looking for jobs. Especially roof cleaning jobs. We were the largest roof and exterior soft washing company in Florida and growing. We ran employment ads, did job fairs, and worked with our local unemployment office to round up candidates for our lead technician positions.

One day, a young man from the local high school walked in our door. This kid was just that, a kid. In fact, he was as green as they get, eighteen years old and fresh off the graduation stage. He asked if we were hiring. "Absolutely we are, absolutely." He completed his application and requested an interview. I jumped right to it because we needed team members. This was basically the interview.

1. Does working outside bother you?
2. Are you afraid of heights?
3. Do you have a clean driving record?
4. Do you have a pulse?

Welcome to the family!

This kid was a rock star from the beginning. A bit green, a bit undisciplined, but this kid had a work ethic. He was hungry, and I could certainly work with hungry.

After a couple of weeks, he shared that he had a friend that was also looking for work and would like to come by and apply. I said, "Sure, have him come by and see me." Well, another green, fresh off the graduation stage, hungry and eager kid appeared. He was also a hustler. My interest was piqued, and I immediately saw a pattern. This initial kid and his buddy were from the same peer group and the same high school. I saw an opportunity to REPLICATE this success.

This caused me to look at my budget for hiring and the expense of the turn-over and retraining cycle I was facing. I derived a plan to bonus a team member if they brought in a new candidate to work at my company. If they stayed at least 90-days, I would bonus the referring team member $500.00.

Within a few short months, we had ten of this initial kid's friends working for us. We went from beating our heads against the wall looking for employees to full-up with great team members. In fact, it was working so well for everyone involved that great things started happening. The kind of things that only happen when you REPLICATE and not automate.

It was an awesome time of growth. The business grew, and the team members grew in their personal lives. I had eighteen- and nineteen-year-old kids making $45,000 a year cleaning roofs. Buying cars. Getting married. Craziest of all, one of these kids at nineteen years old bought his first house before I even had purchased my own home. I had found a way to REPLICATE a result to fill my employment gap and, at the same time, touch and bless a bunch of kids just coming out of school.

As my company grew, I also understood the power of REPLICATION when it comes to the standardization of resources. I had built an exterior cleaning company based upon a unique and innovative approach called soft washing. This equipment was very different than pressure washing equipment, and the trucks were equipped and stocked to do cleanings that were best suited for soft washing. I learned quickly that trucks and crews that were not identically equipped were a stumbling block when it came to training and even booking work.

Highly-replicable; highly-systemized, identical trucks like the one shown above owned by Madison SoftWash from Madison, Wisconsin

If the trucks are not identically equipped, then it makes it almost impossible to develop a training system that you can send every employee through and REPLICATE the same result. Additionally, it became a huge headache if trucks had differing capacities, differing equipment, differing team capabilities when it came time to schedule the jobs. You no longer could simply dispatch work based upon geographical location. You had to consider equipment, capacity, and capability as well. Scheduling became a nightmare if any of these considerations were not a match with the job suited best for a geographical route.

This is how I solved that problem.

1. All lead technicians and assistants had to be certified under our training system.
2. All trucks had to have identical soft wash systems on the trucks with identical capabilities.

3. All work was to fit into our model for how our trucks were equipped. Work that did not fit our model was turned away.

We took all of our trucks and converted them to identical little ducklings that, in a row, you could not see a bit of difference between the others. In a nutshell, we REPLICATED our trucks and focused on the work they were designed to accomplish.

Three trucks became six trucks. Six trucks became twelve trucks, and finally, twelve trucks became eighteen trucks. In the year 2000, we had eighteen service trucks soft washing in three branches across Florida, producing revenues of 4.8 million dollars a year. That is a $267,000 average truck per year, day-in and day-out, regardless of turnover, weather, or breakdowns. We only achieved that by standardizing the trucks and REPLICATING the model.

REPLICATION leads to magnification. In the purest sense, if you want to 10X something as Grant Cardone promotes, you will need to 1X the REPLICABLE model first, then pour gas on that, setting it on fire and blowing it up.

DO NOT READ PAST THAT POINT. You will need to 1x something in order to 10x it. You must get your model down. The first effort is called your proof of concept. Once you have a solid proof of concept and have worked most of the bugs out, then REPLICATE. 10x a papercut and it will become a hemorrhaging wound.

CHAPTER 14

REPLICATION NOT AUTOMATION

REPLICATION is the foundational base of my SoftServ Business System. This is the system I developed to run our 4.8 million dollar a year soft washing company at its height back in the year 2000. In my business system SoftServ, I use the visual of the blending of chocolate and vanilla soft serve ice cream on a cone. It is actually the logo for the business system product.

The vanilla ice cream represents the "old school" visual business systems of your grandparents' generation. Big bold systems posted very visually on walls in the business for rallying the team and creating a high accountability environment.

The chocolate ice cream represents what I call digital chocolate. Digital chocolate is all of these cool computer/ device-based CRMs (customer relationship managers) and other apps that make customer follow-up and drip campaigns easier. The SoftServ System blends the best of both of these worlds, just like a soft-serve swirl ice cream cone.

For a moment, let me address automation. I am not the biggest fan of automation. I am a fan, however. I am in the back row at the concert, and I am not dancing. I conservatively and cautiously embrace automation in all of its forms, especially digital automation.

That being said, I am very progressive in my business views. There is a chasm of difference between automation and progression. I lean far towards progression when it comes to REPLICATION and I do embrace new technology surely. I am simply cautioning you not to automate yourself out of a lasting relationship with your customer.

Here is what I am getting at. Progression as an example is as follows:

Let's say it is the late 1870s, and I own a sawmill. I am a purveyor of fine lumbers and building supplies for our local community. I service a 50-mile radius, which is about two days ride for one of my service carts drawn by mule or oxen.

For me to do business with my clients, they come to me after the design process and visit our mill to examine our product. Our customer places an order for their lumber and other supplies, and we power up the mill, cut their lumber to spec, and deliver that lumber by mule-drawn carriage about 30 days later. I will likely never see the building my lumber was used to build and may not ever engage with that customer again.

The year is now 1886. Alexander Graham Bell has invented and introduced the telephone. I can now "call on" my potential customers, and they can reach out to me without overnight travel. If I am industrious, I might saddle up a horse and ride to visit some of my wealthier customers or more architecturally significant projects, but the likelihood of that is limited by time and travel resources.

However, an invention has come to market here in the early 1900s, the horseless carriage. This invention allows me to reach more customers, visit more sights, and travel to potential customers. Consequently, we bid on new lumber projects. In fact, it has become so easy to travel that often I will visit construction projects and check on their progress, picking up additional opportunities and new business.

Soon, by the 1920s, larger trucks are being developed, and I am able to move my lumber by gas-powered vehicle and not by slower, less reliable mule-powered carts. My customer base and range are being expanded, and I can easily communicate with and visit my customers. The world is certainly getting smaller.

This is an example of technological progression. Technology made it more possible to interact with the lumber mill customers, not detach and automate the customer interaction. I wholeheartedly believe that leveraging technology to automate business processes will limit or reduce customer interaction. This will create an atmosphere of lowest price wins and that my friend, is a slippery slope.

I often see businesspeople that are nonconfrontational. These people will use automation as a crutch so that they do not have to deal with disappointment or conflict. Not only in the sales process but also in the team member accountability systems in their company.

You may have heard that you get the result you model to your employees and customers. I also submit that you will REPLICATE the result you promote in your avoidance and detachment through digital automation. Be very wary of confusing progression versus automation and, for that matter, automation for REPLICATION. I believe the best kind of automation is through physical REPLICATION.

After that tangent, you are surely looking for an example of a SoftServ System REPLICATION principal that you can immediately use in your company. Here is one of my most successful big visual wall systems that you can do immediately to propel your sales team to a 20% increase in sales revenues.

First, let's mention that, yes, I do not like digital automation, so you can reasonably assume (and correctly so) that I am not big on automated digital marketing. I am a sales team guy, through and through. I have used sales teams in every one of my businesses to put wins on the scoreboard that are equal to sales and revenues into the company.

I believe that almost every organization that grows past the million-dollar mark will need a sales team to accomplish that feat. Keeping that team engaged in the game is very important. I have already shared with you about my MVPs, Scoreboards, and Stats program. Now let me share with you my Sales REPLICATION wall.

Remember I have ADD and need systems and processes to guide my businesses and keep me interested in the game. I personally need big visual systems. I create these systems to cover for and adjust for my inadequacies. Managing salespeople can be a real chore.

I noticed early in my career as an entrepreneur that salespeople, at least productive ones, need careful management. Salespeople are like wild stallions. They are great at running the open range and attacking everything with passion. They even push the boundaries a bit and make managing them uncomfortable. This is why immature entrepreneurs often hire poor salespeople. The immature entrepreneur will hire a mild-mannered, easy-to-manage, non-confrontational person who is NOT a salesperson and expect great results from them.

The fact is great salespeople can be a bit of a handful to manage. I needed a system to deploy that would allow me to create a horse race and keep these wild stallions on the track I wanted them to run on. Allowing sales stallions to run free is a recipe for disaster. You absolutely need these pushy salespeople in your company however you will need systems to manage them.

If you outline desired outcomes carefully and give these wild stallions guidelines to play by, you will get about 80% compliance from your sales team. If you give them no guidelines or a track to run you will get 60% or less compliance and that is a grade of F. An unregulated stable of wild stallions will drive you crazy as a business owner and drive you back into the rut of an owner-operator.

I used to be driven crazy by the true producers in my companies. This was completely my fault. I was unprepared for the energy, enthusiasm, and moral gray areas of a wild stallion sales force. I hated the constant managing of people and made the biggest mistake an immature entrepreneur could possibly make. I hired beneath me and sought people for my team that I could easily manage.

You will need to create systems in your business for managing a great team of bridled wild stallions that work towards a common goal. Here is one of these systems which I will profile from my SoftServ Business System.

Sales REPLICATION Wall is certainly a great name. We all want to REPLICATE sales. I have focused you on the ANALYZATION of your efforts so you can prune away behaviors and efforts that do not work and promote the behaviors and efforts that do work. Then you REPLICATE those behaviors and efforts. This big visual wall system, like my Million Dollar Wall Map, will be a culture-building rallying place in your business that will create a High A "accountability" environment.

Pick a wall in or near your sales room that is at least ten feet wide. Dead center on that wall, about seven feet off the ground, hangs a clear plastic 8.5" x 11" wall sign holder in the landscape (horizontal) position. Now to the right and left of that centered wall sign, hang additional wall signs at 24 inches on center for each additional sales team member you have. You should have room for five total sales team members.

Under each wall sign holder, screw two drywall anchors into the wall, five inches off-center and two inches underneath the wall sign holder. Place a black drywall screw in each of the drywall anchors, LIGHTLY screwed in. Now, purchase some lightweight black chain found in most hardware stores. You will need 60 feet of chain total. Cut the chain into ten six-foot sections. Then unscrew each black drywall screw and add the six-foot chain to the screw and screw it into the drywall anchor. You will now have five wall signs equally spaced down the wall with two six-foot black chains hanging under each.

This next step will require you to purchase some binder clips from an office supply. The sizes you will need will be the small and medium sizes. You will need 150 of each size clip. Then once you have the clips connect 30 small binder clips to the left chain under each wall sign holder and 30 medium size clips to the right chain. This will be a tedious process because you have to remove one side of each clip's handles and loop them through the chain, reconnecting them back to the clip. Make sure each clip is equally spaced down the chain with three or so chain links between each clip until you reach the bottom of the six-foot chain.

Over the top of the wall sign holders, create a banner that says SALES REPLICATION WALL to identify the system and the result you are looking for, REPLICATING.

The wall sign holders are for the identification of the sales rep and the territory they serve. I have included a format shown in the illustration on this page. Add their name, a picture, their territory name, and a map of their territory and/or the zip codes they serve.

The chains below are identified as:

On the left is the leads chain where you place the paper copy of the lead that was taken and paged out to the salesperson (lead sheet).

On the right is where the rep will hang a copy of each quote that has been completed for every lead that hangs on the leads chain. (pink copy)

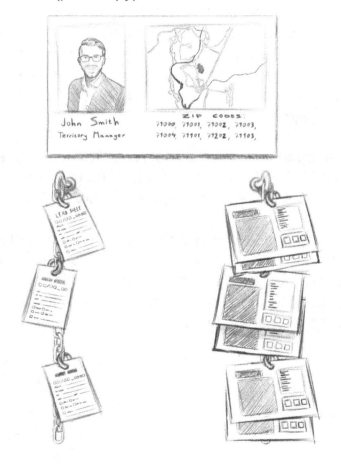

In the SoftServ Business System program, we use printed lead sheets as well as six-part NCR carbonless proposal forms. The NCR proposal forms have six copies to them. White, green, yellow, blue, pink, and gold. I wish I had more time to tell you about these colors and what they mean, but you will need to visit the website for more information on the full SoftServ System program.

Once completed, the pink copy of the quote is brought back to the office and hung onto the right chain. At this point, you will hopefully have at least as many pinks on the quote chain as you have leads on the leads chain. Are you grasping the visual of five reps leads and pinks chains growing throughout the week as leads come in and pinks show the leads have been addressed?

Can you see how this becomes a living bar graph on the wall of your sales room? The visual of how many leads have come in, what salespersons have received those leads, and how they covered those leads is huge when it comes to accountability.

Imagine now you introduce the REPLICATION concept. You now coach and hold your team accountable to not only cover their leads but REPLICATE those leads. It is a Matthew 25 concept. In Matthew 25, the three servants were given talents (money or opportunities) according to their ability.

When the master returned, there were two types of servants revealed. Those who did what was expected and no more, or those who REPLICATED the talent. The parable goes on to describe how happy the master was with the servants that REPLICATED the talent and brought back to the master more than what he had entrusted them with. The parable then turns to the servant that only received one talent.

That servant, in fear of his master's disappointment (and I bet some laziness), dug a hole in the ground and buried the talent, awaiting the return of his master. When the master returned, the servant dug that talent up and hurried back to his master saying, "Master, I didn't screw up. I didn't lose your talent. I played it safe and brought you back exactly what you entrusted me with." The master was angered because the servant only did the minimum expected work. The master cast the servant out saying, "You evil and wicked servant." That servant did not REPLICATE.

This will be so of many of your sales team over the years. Merely just covering their sales leads is lazy. It is a waste of talent and resources. It is the minimum expected and, thereby, doesn't honor the opportunity. This Sales REPLICATION Wall will quickly reveal who is squandering the opportunities/leads your company is providing them.

There is much more to this Sales REPLICATION Wall system I'd love to share. However, just the horse race and living bar graph this will create in your business will encourage not only covering of the leads but also the additional effort of REPLICATION.

In my businesses, we require a 2/1 REPLICATION effort. This means that for every lead that comes into the sales team and is posted to a sales team member's chains, they must produce two quotes. One quote to cover the lead that came in through the business and another quote from their personal efforts while out running the company lead. This has proven highly effective over the years. This

REPLICATES their efforts and multiplies the results of our sales and marketing programs.

Here is the math. If a sales team member receives ten leads in a week and closes 80% of those leads with an average quote of $1,000, then those ten leads generate $8,000 in revenues.

AUTOMATOR'S MATH

10 leads × 80% CR = 8 closed jobs
8 closed jobs × $1000 Average Jobs = $8000 Revenue

*CR — closing ratio

If that same sales team member, then walks across the street and knocks on a few doors and gets one other resident to allow them to provide a quote, you might REPLICATE those ten leads into twenty. Now you have REPLICATED your potential business to $20,000 in quotes. If you have a 50% closing ratio (less than you had with the original ten leads) and a $1,000 average quote, that sales team member will produce $10,000 in closed sales. That is a 20% increase by applying REPLICATION.

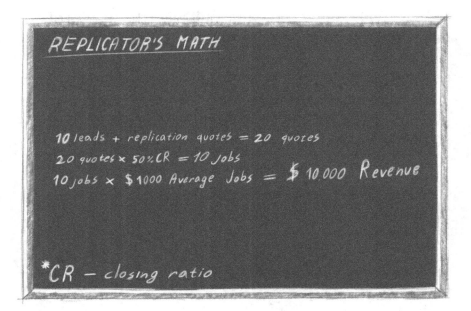

REPLICATOR'S MATH

10 leads + replication quotes = 20 quotes
20 quotes × 50% CR = 10 Jobs
10 jobs × $1000 Average Jobs = $10,000 Revenue

*CR — closing ratio

If you also consider the visual impact to your office this wall will make, the competitive culture it will create, and the quick ANALYZATION you can do by merely walking by the highly visual SYSTEM, you can realize the impact this High Accountability SYSTEM can have on your success. I encourage you to look more closely into my SoftServ Business SYSTEM by following this QR code shown here so you can REPLICATE more results like these.

www.ProBizGuide.com/SoftServ/

THE FIFTH KEY - SYSTEMIZE

CHAPTER 15

THE REPLICATION OF MY REPLICATION IS MY SYSTEM

You have very likely heard the saying, "The enemy of my enemy is my friend." The premise of this statement is that your enemy has an enemy, and if you befriend your enemy's enemy, then the two of you have a common goal together, to crush your mutual enemy. It is what is called a circular statement. It is much like the statement "Two wrongs don't make a right, but three lefts do." These are statements that make us laugh and then think a little. When I say "the replication of my replication is my system," it is to be jovial and thought-provoking.

In all of these statements, there is a DUH factor, the blatant, in-your-face truth that seems so simple but very few actually grasp. "The enemy of my enemy," "Three lefts," or "The REPLICATION of my REPLICATION." These small statements make you slap yourself on the forehead and say, "DUH". SYSTEMS are just the REPLICATION of your best REPLICATORS. The special sauce in your business that you want to do more of. In a good way, the automation of the REPLICABLE positive result, so that you can get more of the good results over and over without the initial huge effort it took to accomplish the goal. You have a machine that capitalizes on momentum and REPLICATES the desired result over and over again.

I know I sound like I am contradicting myself in the previous sections rant against digital automation. I assure you I am not, and here is why. I like to automate results that do not require human interaction in the form of relationship building. I firmly believe that many people are being led away from human interaction first by fear and second by laziness. As I have said, I believe many lean upon the crutch of automation. That is not to say that automation is bad. It is a useful tool.

Marcus Lemonis, the CEO of Camping World and the TV show "The Profit," talks about his Three Ps: People, Product, and Process. Let's look at his Three P's in some detail. Yes, these are out of order to make a point.

AC softwashing a shingle roof, 1994

The Replication of My Replication is My System

Process

Processes can be automated or organic. Organic is where you have guidelines and protocols for completing a process in your business but not through automation. Albeit, either is fine here because processes are not human. They do not require a relationship. They do not get their feelings hurt or need affirmation. Processes are procedures you put in place to bring a product or service to market. These processes need to be clean and mathematical in nature. Automation is fine here.

Product

If you make and sell a widget, it is very easy to automate the manufacturing process. In a service business, this becomes more difficult. Automating a service has to be a simple deliverable.

For instance, there are companies out in the marketplace that automate the customer review process. Literally, they put an automated digital system in place that helps to drive more reviews to your social media channels without you having to lift a single finger. These service automation opportunities are rare.

In a consumer services business, you are likely selling labor. You can hedge that labor with great processes, great training, great tools, and great support; however, you are invested in a flesh-based product. People doing business with people with a service performed by people for a person in a home or business.

A great example of a poor implementation of automation where people are involved can be found in how many companies today address customer care after the sale. Have you ever needed support on a product and called "customer no service"? You might have been sent into "press 2" for Purgatory. A menu of options that you press "1" for English, "3" for support, "2" for live support, only to be forwarded to a foreign call center where agents speak poorly, and their knowledge is limited to the same FAQ (frequently asked questions) database you had access to all along. Don't even get me started on mega conglomerates like GOOGLE who only use an FAQ and have blocked any and all human interaction of any kind with their customers.

People

Marcus puts forth the theory that you cannot have just two of these three P's in a business. You must have all three in equal amounts to be successful. As an ingredient in a successful business in equal amounts, you must have quality ingredients to result in a quality product. Quality is key. Having quality people makes everything in your business go better. You engage with four types of people in your business. It is important to recognize that these four divisions exist.

Employees – the people who join your team and work with you.
Customers – the people who buy your product or service.
Suppliers – the people who sell you raw materials or services.
Regulators – the people who hold you accountable to the laws.

There is no possible way for you to automate these relationships without receiving a diminishing return. Now, I know some of you are saying "But, AC, I can set an alert on my calendar to remind me of a birthday or anniversary so I can order a gift or send a note to a client, and that is automation." And I would wholeheartedly agree with you. However, if a person/client you cared for only ever heard from you by automated response, they would begin to wonder if you had a genuine appreciation for their business.

In other words, how good would your relationship be with your wife if you ticked all of the boxes, remembered her birthday, sent a gift, remembered your anniversary, sent a gift, provided income, sent a check, paid college bill for kids, sent a check. You could say you were a good spouse in that you checked all of the boxes on a form, couldn't you?

However, your spouse would have a different version of the story. [Fill in the blank] _____ was a good provider, but they never truly listened to me. We never went out on dates, and they never picked up the phone to say hello or check on me. Human interaction cannot be automated, and this is a necessary soft skill you will need to develop in your business.

We do this well at SoftWash Systems. One of the full-time positions in our company is the position of Relationship Manager. This team member's job is to manage the client experience with SoftWash Systems through real personal engagement.

As best as we can at SoftWash Systems we track and keep aware of birthdays, anniversaries, births, illnesses, deaths, hospitalizations, and the like. We send flowers, make phone calls and interact at varying levels to make sure our in-network companies know we value them.

This team member also handles compliance for our company. They are judge and jury on in-network companies qualifying each year to remain in or be offboarded from our organization. They handle accountability to our 50-Point Standard and Code of Conduct. They are the Yin and the Yang of Love and Accountability in our organization.

The caring approach of sending a baby gift for a birth or flowers to a funeral must be done in a non-automated and caring way. Without that, you have no authority to hold that person or company accountable when a tough discussion must be had.

Human beings can systemize processes without automating them undoubtedly. I am warning all of you to be careful what you automate and understand the difference between a system and an automation in your business. Do not become cold and calculated removing the human experience and thereby product loyalty.

Alright, now that you know where I stand on where and when automation is okay and how automation might play into SYSTEMATIZATION, let's look at the definitions of SYSTEMS before we move forward.

SYSTEM
A set of things working together as parts of a mechanism or an interconnecting network.

SYSTEMATIC
Done or acting according to a fixed plan or system; methodical.

SYSTEMATIZATION
Arrange according to an organized system; make systematic.

I want you to merge all three of these uses or definitions together to describe your SYSTEMATIZATION process.

OUR SYSTEMIZE DEFINITION
To arrange a process, defined by a set of steps, in a fixed plan, to achieve a series of replicated results.

Four specific types of systems are generally recognized in engineering: **product systems, service systems, enterprise systems, and system of systems**.

PRODUCT SYSTEMS

Systems that you might put into place when addressing process needs in your products might be related to innovation, manufacturing, support, and go-to-market. These systems for product development must be followed in this order. You will need to have these systems in place in your business, or as you grow, your business will collapse in on itself.

The product innovation cycle is the lifeblood of a growing/flourishing company. Innovation not only gives you new products to sell, but it sends a message to your customers that your company is leading and evolving. Here is where your company's product ideas are born, engineered, and developed into a prototype.

MANUFACTURING SYSTEMS

Manufacturing SYSTEMS can be processes but also equipment lines. Here, your prototype is broken down into REPLICABLE sub-systems or assemblies that are individually duplicated to form the compiled end product. Here, you will take your prototype and make decisions like "Is this a make or buy part?" In other words, is this something we will make from scratch, or is this something we can engage a subcontractor or supplier on? Also, considerations of buying new equipment, adding new employees, adding more warehouse space. You will need a written SYSTEM for producing or manufacturing this new product offering.

ENTERPRISE SYSTEMS

The enterprise area of your business is where you SYSTEMIZE processes like sales, marketing, ordering, product delivery, shipping, and billing. Enterprise SYSTEMS handle the flow of capitalizing on your product and or service, producing and selling it to the public, and monetizing the result.

I like to think about the OLD SCHOOL "Schoolhouse Rock" series that was on Saturday mornings when I was a kid. You can search for these on YouTube. One of my favorites was I'm Just a Bill. Though this Schoolhouse Rock video was about how a bill became a law, it did do a great job explaining processes. The steps from idea, to invention, to acceptance. You can take that video and input any concept or idea. Kind of like a fill in the blank, I'M JUST A _____. Knowing how to monetize an idea is the purist form of capitalism.

GO-TO-MARKET SYSTEMS

Merely inventing a product is not enough. You need to know how to bring a product to market. The first time you do this as a solopreneur it is easy. You are likely your only employee, and you make all of the decisions. Soon you will be successful and have a team. How do you pull your

The Replication of My Replication is My System

team into the go-to-market process to lighten your load? You will need a SYSTEM in place that outlines the steps to bring a new product to market.

This is completely different from enterprise SYSTEMS where you are monetizing the product. Go-to-market systems follow this short process once the product is completed in engineering, prototype, and manufacturing. Here is an example I have used in my businesses:

1. Trials or In-field Testing

Here, you engage third-party companies or trusted industry insiders to test your product to affirm it does what you promote it to do. Also, here, you hope to work the bugs out before it goes to market.

2. Market Study

This is as simple as asking yourself how big the market is and what will be the need for your widget. It is a hard question to ask because as entrepreneurs, we get emotionally attached to an idea or product. We never want to see one of our children (products or ideas) fail, let alone possibly choose to put one to death. Some great products serve such a small subset of the overall market that they are very useful to a few but so few of the products cannot be monetized. Remember there are no bad ideas; however, there are few you can support a family on.

3. Marketing Assessment

Once you know who your target client is and that the group is large enough to monetize, then you need to strategize how to reach that group with marketing. Now is the time to get ahead of your production and create the buzz so that orders outpace production. It is also the time where you will create a budget for marketing this new product. Pick the advertising sources. Target the start of the advertising program. Study the seasonality of how you will market the product or service.

4. <u>Sales Development</u>

When the phone starts ringing, you will need to know how to close the deal and process the order. This all falls onto the sales department. Will you be online or in stores? Will you go direct to the consumer? Do you need a sales team, or can you automate by processing orders online? A small product can be purchased from a website, but a service or higher ticket item may need a consultant or even a sales visit. Now is the time to decide what your sales process might look like. Develop three paths to sell your product or service. Automobile sales today are a great place to find inspiration. Literally, you can buy a car 100% online and have it dropped at your door. Or you can browse from the comfort of your home, finding three to five best candidates, and then go visit those dealers in person. Finally, you can jump in your current car and hit "car row," and buzz in here-and-there looking at cars. Meet and pick a sales representative. Walk the lots, physically looking over each and every car. You can see there are three completely different sales experiences here for three differing personalities, but these are called purchasing channels. And three fishing rods in the water catch more fish than just one.

5. Support Development

Once you bring a new product or service to market, you will need to support that product or service after the sale. You will need to develop a user's manual. Produce a technical support web page. Create a frequently asked questions (FAQ) or knowledge base on your website. Hire phone support for call-in technical support or customer care claims.

6. Legacy Process

What I mean by legacy is, hopefully, your product or service will either be long-lasting or be regularly needed. Nothing is forever, and your clients need to know if your product or service has a warranty. Where do you go to buy repair parts? How do you submit a claim? How long should the product last? Will the product become unsupported, if ever? Will there be a version two or any upgrades?

This is the time to dream about the future of your product or service. It is good to establish a timeline looking out 24 months, five years, seven years to see if you can engage the client into the culture of the product and have them grow in acceptance of the product evolution as the previous products wear out or become non-supported.

CHAPTER 16

FOR THOSE ABOUT TO ROCK

A Rock flyer

I first discovered the power of converting REPLICABLE results into a SYSTEMIZED process in the early 1990s. I, maybe like you, was a solopreneur and was wearing a lot of hats in my company. The economy was slow and even worse I had not developed my target avatar customer as of then. I was literally walking through neighborhoods and hanging door hangers to generate business.

I had honed the hanging of door hanger literature to an art. I had studied door hangers from other service companies and had split test door hangers so I could study the results between one door hanger's content against another. I had discovered the hole atop the door hanger flyer was difficult to place on door handles. It was cumbersome and noisy. I had even had a gun shoved in my face one day as I was hanging a door hanger, jiggling the handle from the effort, and the door swung open. As I looked up anxiously, a large man stood in his doorway with a handgun drawn, yelling for me to get off his property. I also noticed that the door hanger hole took up a great amount of real estate on the door hanger that I could use for a message or pictures. So, I deleted the hole from my door hangers and created a rack card.

A rack card had many more uses. I could use them for home and garden shows; I could leave them at hardware stores; I could give them to realtors. For doors, I noticed if I printed them on a thicker stock that I could easily slide the rack card between the door and jamb weather stripping, quickly avoiding noise or fidgeting. Just this one simple solution saved time and created a better advertising product.

I would clean in the mornings and walk neighborhoods in the afternoon, placing hundreds of these rack cards on potential customers' doors. On average, I would receive one call for every one hundred rack cards distributed to doors. This was time-consuming and had a low yield of leads to rack cards ratio distributed, in light of the time expended to accomplish the task. However, I was getting my name out, and it did result in enough business to keep me and my one truck busy.

As I grew my company, I added more service trucks. I alone could not keep the flow of leads coming into the company by merely distributing rack cards. I did notice that rack cards gave me a consistent result of 1/100 calls to rack cards distributed. I was only one person, and if I was going to grow my business and increase my income, I would need to REPLICATE myself and SYSTEMIZE the sales effort.

The most basic but certainly not easiest way to grow a business is to develop a sales team. Basically, you are taking everything you do in a day to market your business, run those leads, close those sales, and clone yourself into a team of people who can REPLICATE what you do.

If you could distribute 400 rack cards a day, generate four leads, close two of those leads at $750 each, generating $1,500 in sales each day, then four clones of you can generate $6,000 in sales a day. It is a no-brainer.

This does not come without risk, and I need to explain why. Many fledgling companies have owners that are afraid to sell or just downright don't like it. Most owners are more comfortable with the process of doing the technical aspect of their business and avoiding customer interaction. (Remember my rant on digital automation.)

The average business owner will think hiring a salesperson is such a great move that they skip the selling process themselves all together. The owner never serves any period of time in the growth of the business in the sales department and immediately delegates this off to a new hire salesperson. Let me assure you, that is the kiss of death for any small business.

Here is why. To create a sales team, you will need to set aside base salary and commissions from the proceeds of the product or service you are selling. Generally, this will account for ten to fifteen percent of your gross revenues. You must understand that if you are not profitable or have very little profit before adding a salesperson, you will certainly have less to no profit afterward.

A general rule before adding a salesperson is that your company needs to be in the fifty percent or better net profit range to afford a salesperson. If you are living check to check now or have a small ten percent profit, you simply cannot afford a sales team. You will need to raise your prices in order to grow your business. The key to growing all businesses is to raise prices every time.

Now imagine a situation where your company is in pretty good shape. You actually have a thirty percent net profit. You're super profitable, right? Actually, you're in trouble.

To pay a salesperson is ten to fifteen percent of the gross revenues. Also, you will find that until your salesperson is fully trained and knows the product, they will likely undersell. The facts are salespersons who are not owners sell an average of fifteen to twenty percent under value than the business owner will.

This can happen for several reasons. First, the customers like dealing with owners and respect the owners and do not hammer them for discounts. Second, salespeople do not have a concept of the cost or value of the product/service and what it likely takes to produce that product/service. They are more closely paying attention to the commission generated in relation to their paycheck. On average, a job sold by a salesperson will be twenty-five to thirty percent lower gross revenue as compared to an owner-generated sale. So be prepared for the fact that adding a salesperson will reduce gross revenues by as much as 30%.

Now that you know the risk, you need to be DELIBERATE and formulate a plan before building a sales team. Training, mentoring, equipping, and holding them accountable is a full-time job, and you will likely be their boss, the sales manager. Once you are ready to build that team and REPLICATE yourself, you will scale quickly.

Back to the rack cards. I now had four salespersons in my company. I can tell you this ... they were not as hungry as I was. Let's face it. If they were, they would have built and owned their own company. I expected my sales team to go out and distribute the same amount of rack cards as I did every day. They never did. At best, I would get 70% compared to my personal effort. Then once you factored in all of the walking and the Florida heat six months out of the year, our numbers were falling off fast.

One day, I was at home and needed to go out to check my mail. As I walked up my driveway, I noticed a small zip-lock-style baggie on my driveway with something in it. I picked it up and noticed that there was a business card inside of the bag and a small scoop of gravel. I realized someone was literally driving around in their air-conditioned car, tossing out these baggies onto people's driveways and getting out hundreds of them a day.

Bang! The light went on in my head. What if I could take my proven 1/100 rack cards, put them in a bag, add a couple of rocks ... Now, we were cooking. I now had a plan to get out thousands of what we now call rock flyers to REPLICATE the 1/100 result and keep my sales team in leads.

Eventually, these rock flyers would become the staple of our marketing efforts, distributing around nine thousand pieces a month. Creating over 90 leads for my sales team. Generating in excess of $68,000 in proposals that, at a 80% closing ratio, was over $54,000 in gross revenues.

Additionally, this was just one marketing channel alone. These rock flyers were the birth of something special that was developed the months following, and today is a marketing SYSTEM that has generated hundreds of millions of dollars in soft wash cleaning revenues worldwide.

CHAPTER 17
A MOVIE AND SOME POPCORN

The famous radio personality Paul Harvey of the radio show The Rest of the Story, said it best when describing marketing. I heard him once say, "You have to reach a customer with three or more forms of advertising before your brand and message really sinks in and they buy." King Solomon in the book of Ecclesiastes (4:12) in wisdom said, "A chord of many strands is not easily broken." In marketing, you need to have a multi-pronged approach to have true influence over your suspected client base.

What I developed over the years is a SYSTEM called Popcorn Marketing. My Popcorn Marketing is the only thing I have found that creates REPLICABLE marketing success over and over. It is mathematical and consistent. You can count on the SYSTEM every time. It has worked in the United States as well as in the United Kingdom and even Europe. It works regardless of regulations or culture. It simply works every time we have deployed it.

To date, in our businesses and the businesses that emulate our practices, Popcorn Marketing has produced nearly a billion dollars in sales worldwide. This advertising SYSTEM did not stop at the rock flyer. Around the simple rock flyer, I built a SYSTEMIZED approach of boots-on-the-ground advertising I came to call Popcorn Marketing.

Popcorn Marketing, in its essence, is defined as simple effective marketing done in bursts. These bursts are not to be confused with canvasing. Popcorn marketing is meant to be small but measurable. Marketing you do alongside your trade. Little bursts while heading to a lead. Little bursts while leaving a job. Little bursts that are easily REPLICABLE throughout your workday so that you accomplish a great deal of marketing before you realize it.

The visual of a bag of popcorn kernels exploding while each individual kernel pops to fill the bag. In the same way, you will do "pops" of marketing while you go along your workday. Not in any particular order like canvassing, however where you find yourself during your workday in a smaller, more random covering. Like the bag of popcorn expanding and filling one pop at a time, you will find yourself covering your territory one pop at a time.

In my Popcorn Marketing approach, we leverage several tools. Here is a comprehensive list and how they work.

Rack Cards/Rock Flyers

As mentioned in the previous chapter, I was faced with the task of keeping my sales team in their territory and keeping them busy marketing. Door hangers worked okay; however, I soon found and perfected something so much more. Placing a rack card in a bag along with a rock or two is certainly not earth-shattering by itself. However, when done at a rate of 3,500 a week or more, word gets out, and the phone begins to ring.

Today, many call these rock flyers or clip flyers "Popcorn Marketing." The fact is it is only one spoke in a multi-spoked system for Popcorn Marketing. Popcorn Marketing can literally be any form of marketing that you can do in small bursts or "pops", a bit at a time while you carry on with your day. Rock flyers are great because you can distribute these flyers from the comfort of your air conditioned vehicle.

Yard Signs

Yard signs have been a staple of the service business industry for decades. These signs can be elaborate or quite simple. One color or full color. Square or die-cut to a shape. Disposable or worthy of reuse.

The basic idea of a yard sign is the forced referral. A referral is when a neighbor tells another about the great service you provided. This might take a day to happen, a week, or never happen at all. The fact is happy customers are rarely moved to brag about your service. They received what you promised without trouble or issues and went back to their grind and forgot about you. A forced referral is where you tell the neighbor you did a great job (through placing a yard sign) and encourage the neighbor to engage your customer and ask about your service or product.

Yard signs should be brand-centric. I often use the term message over branding. Message over branding is the term used where you make the focus of your advertising piece your message, not your brand. Yard signs should be branding over message. The logo should be at the top and not the message.

The truth is, my first company, Mallard Systems became well known by our brand and what we provided as a service. So well-known that I could just put our duck on a stick in the yard with no message, and everyone knew what was done.

The yard sign just made the statement that Mallard Systems had soft washed another roof. Of course, please add your message and contact information below your logo, but nothing more than that. I did a ten-year study on our marketing, and for every yard sign we placed out, we got one new project in return.

Check-It-Out Flyers

A check-it-out flyer is a simple 1/3 sheet flyer on color paper with black ink. It is very simple for a reason. The rack card/rock flyer you threw in the drive of the house was full color on glossy stock. The yard sign was full color on a glossy board. It's time to change it up. The check-it-out flyer should be different so as to elicit a reaction.

Much like a yard sign, it is a forced referral. On the check-it-out flyer, you should have on the top: YOUR NEIGHBOR AT _____ HAS HAD THESE SURFACES SOFT WASHED. You fill in the address of the home you soft washed. Then below that is a list of the services you provide and boxes alongside them. This is a message over branding piece. For the home you just serviced, check the boxes that apply to the services you rendered. This crude flyer communicates to the customer what you did for their neighbor. If you're lucky, it will also create a "Keeping up with the Joneses" competition amongst neighbors.

Once a service job is completed, you will distribute six of these flyers to the front doors of neighbors. One flyer to the right and the left of the home you just serviced and four across the street. If on a given service day you have three appointments, you will distribute 18 of these Check-It-Out flyers. This is Popcorn Marketing at its essence.

Truck/Vehicle Wraps

The most important piece of real estate you have is your service truck or other company vehicles. These vehicles can become moving billboards. You already own them, so they might as well be working for you.

While on the way into the neighborhood, neighbors will see your truck and its branding. While on the job site, each neighbor that drives by will see the wrap as well. On your return to the shop, neighbors and others in the community will see your work vehicle.

A truck wrap will get you many impressions. An impression is an advertising term used to measure the effectiveness of getting your advertising in front of people. This is used widely in TV and radio advertising. Vehicle wraps will account for nearly 20% of all of your requests for proposals.

Sublimated Shirts/Uniforms

Much like a vehicle wrap, a sublimated shirt is like wrapping your body. Literally, you can have a company take the same graphics and files from your truck wrap and create a matching full-color shirt for you to wear. These are super effective for branding and differentiation. You can get polo–styled, collared ones for managers and salespeople, and crew neck-style ones for technicians.

As I mentioned, I was a professional fisherman from 2005–2009, winning the Redfish Tour National Championship in 2006. In 2006, everyone wore heavy cotton, long-sleeved shirts with heavy non-breathable embroidery all over them for sponsor logos, etc. In 2007, I was asked by the tour to pilot a new program for a new tour sponsor who did sublimation fishing jerseys. These jerseys came from the cycling world.

I was the first angler in the United States to fish a tournament in a sublimated uniform. They were light, air flowed through them, and they were indestructible. Later in 2008, I realized if these shirts were so good for the tour, looking great and matching the boat and truck wraps, then they would work just as well for my sales team at my cleaning company. It was amazing how quickly I found out how much roof cleaning you could sell standing in line at a Seven-Eleven.

Radius Bombs

I am not a fan of direct mail. It has never been successful for me. However, a cool new product came out in 2016 from a company called Send Jim. The product is called a radius bomb. I now encourage all of my in-network companies at SoftWash Systems to Radius Bomb every job they do. Here is how it works.

A Radius Bomb is a form of my dreaded direct mail, but it is highly focused and effective. It is accomplished with a postcard style mailing to a pre-defined group of target customers. The way the postcards are deployed is how the bomb works.

Send Jim has an app that you can load onto your device. In the app, you can pre-load various postcards and other mailings. On the postcards, you can customize them with pictures or differing messages. The postcard I recommend for doing a Radius Bomb is a hybrid between a check-it-out flyer and a before & after picture advertising. The postcard template on your app will have a spot defined for uploading your before and after pictures and the address of the home you serviced.

Once you have completed your project and have uploaded a compelling before and after photo, completing the address info as well, you're ready to bomb that area. The app allows you to enter that home or business address, then pinch/pull a radius bubble around your completed project. As you pinch/pull, you can see the number of target mailers that will go out. I like to settle on the closest 100 homes, then bombs away.

It Is a Fool-Proof System

Think about what we just accomplished with these six Popcorn Marketing ingredients. Watch this pop and explode.

On the way into the service job, you throw one hundred rock flyers on the right-hand side of the road. The neighbors also see your truck. You arrive at the home or business you are servicing and place out a yard sign. The entire time you are servicing the home or business, neighbors drive by and notice you and you're cleaning. When completed, you place six check-it-out flyers on the doors of the homes to the right, left, and four across the street. You complete your before and after pictures, and upload them to the Send Jim app from where you Radius Bomb one hundred of the closest homes and businesses around the project you just completed. On the way out of the neighborhood, you rock flyer one hundred homes on the left side of the road. Do you realize how easy that was and what you have accomplished?

If you use the math above and complete six projects a week:

Six projects driving in = Six hundred rock flyers
Six projects seeing your wrapped truck driving around
Six Yard Signs
Six projects of Check-It-Out Flyers = 36 Check-It-Outs
Six Projects bombed = 600 reached by Radius Bomb
Six projects driving out = Six Hundred Rock Flyers

Stop to get gas and a drink at Seven-Eleven = Sublimated Shirt Bonus

This helps SYSTEMIZE the REPLICATION principal now. If you sell one job and Popcorn Market off of it as explained above, you will generate six to ten leads every time your truck leaves the shop to complete the next service job.

I have taught this system to companies for nearly twenty years now. I have no real numbers or a third-party study to boast, but I have heard many, many testimonies of businesses tripling their revenues using the Popcorn Marketing system. That's 300% growth from this one SYSTEM.

If you know you can REPLICATE a good result and you can do it repeatedly, you need to develop a SYSTEM around that REPLICABLE result. Layers of simple systems in a business will achieve repeatable, REPLICABLE, and reliable results, creating freedom in your business as well as in your personal life.

THE LOCKS, THE KEYS, THE ORDER

CHAPTER 18

UNLOCK THE POTENTIAL, IGNORE THE PAST

You are likely enthused about these Five Keys and ready to go; however, your old demons and doubts may be prodding you in the background.

AC and Tom Ziglar, CEO of Ziglar International. (proud son of the legend, Zig Ziglar)

"AC is a freak of nature; you can't be like him."

"He doesn't know your past, your secrets. You're damaged goods. Flawed in every way."

"There is no way you can do this. You're not smart enough."

That is not true. Do not listen to those demons. You can rise above them. Yes, my life reads like a storybook in many areas. However, I could tell my personal story in a much different way that might shock you.

Did you know that I am a hot mess? I am a resounding example of imperfection and weakness. My list of accomplishments is only overshadowed by my list of failures. If I was to tell you my story from the perspective of my failures, you would think I was doomed. So many people will build your perception of them by building their story based upon their highlight reel of successes. Let me tell you my story through the lens of my struggles.

I was born in Miami Beach, Florida, in 1969 to my parents Al and Janice Lockyer. I was an only child (at least for the first 13 years of my life. When I was thirteen and fifteen, my parents and I adopted two beautiful baby girls, and I became a brother.) I was loved, cared for, and given everything my parents could possibly and reasonably provide for me. I was white, middle class, and had a life ahead of me, full of opportunity.

I was a happy child. I would sing and dance all of the time. Life for me was a constant musical. I loved all people, didn't see color, and grew up unbiased. I was a part of the Sesame Street generation. My family spent time together going on vacations, fishing almost every Saturday or Sunday, and investing in activities like Cub Scouts or ball sports.

I started school in kindergarten like many. However, because I was a September baby, I was always the oldest kid in my class. Immediately in the pecking order of popularity, which happens early in elementary school, I was singled out by bullies and marginalized.

I was not very athletic. In fact, I was usually the last kid picked at recess in that schoolyard pick for teams. In my peer groups I would settle into, I was always third or fourth in the perceived chain of friendship. There was always the cool kid, then his or her best friend, then the third wheel, then little Alfie.

As I entered first grade, I started to fall behind quickly, as far as academics and social interaction go. In fact, by second grade, my teacher had all but given up on me, relegating me to the back of the room and allowing me to build tents and forts out of extra chairs so she would not have to deal with me. As I mentioned in the introduction of this book, my next-door neighbor Bertha Shouldice, who was a counselor and researcher at Barry University, noticed my struggling and brought me into a program that diagnosed my issue as A.D.D.

By third grade, I was failing many classes. Parent-teacher conferences, summer school, and disappointment became the norm for me at school. I was not quick with math. In fact, I would have described myself as stupid by the middle years of elementary school. That culminated later in me failing the third grade and being held back to repeat the grade. Now, in the eyes of my peers, I was not athletic and stupid to boot.

I was overweight. My parents and clothing manufacturers called it HUSKY. What a label to have at eight years old ... HUSKY. Being an overweight kid, not athletic, and now almost two years older than any other kid in my classes was devastating. However, I still sang and danced. I was still a happy kid, not realizing my social condition because, honestly, I was oblivious with joy and very naive. What happens then is predators start to identify you as weak or wounded, and they stalk and attack you.

My third grade through fifth-grade years (only three years, but for a child, they seemed like a lifetime) were very rough for me. For those in my family who are reading this, they will be shocked. I suffered in silence for the most part from 1978–1980. The attacks were simple at first. The school bully intimidating me during recess. Then they became more progressive, like being beaten almost weekly by kids in the school bathroom while stealing my lunch money. When I did fight back, I was blamed for the violence and silenced once again. I learned early in my life to just take the beating or abuse and say nothing.

I am not sure what I even felt after those years. Numb, I guess. I am not sure how it changed me. I just know when bad things happen, you get a brand burned into your soul, and predators see and sense it. I just knew I became a target fast. For most of my school career, third through seventh grade, I acted out. Many times, defending myself from predators. Other times, doing stupid stuff to gain attention and climb the social ladder. I was overcompensating tremendously.

That all being said, I was now a victim. Victim of violence. Victim of physical abuse. Victim of mental abuse. Victim of bullying. Because of my soft heart and being others-centered, I dared not say anything to anyone and lay that burden upon them. I just kept singing, dancing, and keeping up appearances.

What possibly saved my life was, in 1979, a family we were close with, the Bensons, decided to move from Miami up to Orlando, Florida. My parents were close with Dave and Sharron, so we followed them up about a year later in 1980. Then my best friend's family, the Odells, moved up to Orlando in 1981. What this meant for me was a new school, a new home, and a new start. It was the middle of my fifth-grade year.

I thought Orlando was the country compared to the concrete jungle of Miami. On my first day of school, I dressed in cowboy boots, a shirt, and a hat. After all, it was the early 1980s, the Urban Cowboy period. Man, I was a TARGET. The first morning of the first day, right in line, getting ready to enter the school, the school bully started in on me. He walked over and simply flipped my hat off my head and started to mentally abuse me. I was like, "Here we go again." However, something just came over me. I tore into him like a hedgehog on fire and beat him into the ground. Bam, my first day, my first bully, and I had landed in the principal's office. My father had been called to come pick me up. I was about to be suspended from school on my first day.

Because this was the first experience anyone had with me, especially the administration, I was now labeled a violent bully. After all, look at my resume. I was stupid, husky, held back, older than anyone, from Miami, and an outsider. Being eleven years old in the fifth grade while all of my other friends were already in middle school was tough enough.

Scholastically, many parents reward their kids for good grades. Get an A, get a reward. Get a B, get a smaller reward. I was the kid that got rewards for getting a C. My parents were thrilled to just get through a semester without a parent/teacher conference or the threat of repeating the grade. Are you seeing a theme here?

Once you are on a path like this one, you are almost certainly doomed to have a marginal existence unless ... something major changes. Something HUGE has to intersect with your life to divert this path from despair to "Go forth and prosper."

Now I only tell you this story to establish the fact that I am not privileged. I do not have anything at my disposal that you do not have. I am not using any of my junk as an excuse not to move onward and upward with my life. I have junk, just like you.

I could go on and on with a family history of alcoholism and drug abuse. I could talk about money mismanagement and debt. I could smack you in the face again with more stories of all kinds of abuse. Or tell you about the time I was beat with a cow whip by a neighbor boy. We all have a counter-narrative where things could have gone badly for us. Some rise above that, or some use it as an excuse.

I bring all of this to your attention because, as I mentioned at the beginning of this chapter, if I were to do an accounting of the list of my accomplishments against my list of failures and challenges, one might give me a pass and not judge me for not living a victorious life.

Instead, I learned early on to count my blessings, embrace my opportunities, and throw off the things that so easily entangle me. (Hebrews 12:1-3) You cannot do this without taking a sober accounting (Romans 12:3) of your life and ANALYZING the indicators around you, good and bad, so you can make THE NEXT BEST DECISION that moves you towards your victorious and successful life.

My desire is for you to see my frailties and inadequacies and understand that I have indeed come so far. It is my hope for you to also go far in life and in business and create a legacy of victory. You cannot do that without constant ANALYSIS and understanding of the forces and opportunities around you. You simply cannot captain a ship without spending time on navigation.

More than anything, realize that the rock stars out there in the business world are as flawed as am I. The big difference between the person who takes up the victim mentality and the person who lives victoriously is a single decision away. The decision to be DELIBERATE and dream. EXECUTE small moves to accomplish that dream. ANALYZE those moves, pruning away what did not work and throwing more energy behind what did work. REPLICATE the great stuff that is happening in your life and business. Then finally build a SYSTEM around those desired great efforts so that they can be EXECUTED over and over again.

CHAPTER 19

IMPLEMENTING THE KEYS

Hold up your left hand and face it palm towards you. Look at your hand. Remember the five keys? On your thumb is BE DELIBERATE. Your index finger is EXECUTE. The space between your thumb and index finger is the biggest gap on the digits of your hand. It is also the biggest gap in the execution of the Five Keys to Pattern Success. This is the most difficult step in your success process.

As I mentioned earlier, I have a mentor named Howard Partridge. One of his favorite topics to speak about is how entrepreneurs and people, in general, fail to implement. That gap in our minds, that gap in our actions, that gap between the thumb and index finger is large and hard to overcome. The gap between being DELIBERATE and EXECUTION. Not a single one of the Five Keys will work unless you act and implement. Failure to implement will stop your success in its tracks.

Most people (I hope not you) will read this book and move on, inspired but not likely to implement anything from this book. Some will make notes in the margins and use a highlighter to mark meaningful passages. Others may even tell their team about some of the principles in these pages. Most simply will not act. How can we make sure you are different?

I am shouting this at this very moment … EVERY SINGLE WIN I HAVE HAD IN MY LIFE, I HAVE USED THESE FIVE KEYS. Every single one. This works. It is gravitational. It is a mathematical formula. This is a recipe. All you need to do is put effort behind these keys. The only thing standing between you and using these keys for success is YOU!

Are you not tired? Is it not time to drill down and reach for new heights in your life? This may be the plan of action you need to plot a new course in your life and stop settling for less. You can be successful and have a wonderful life and business. Just apply the formula, the keys. Unlock your better decisions and open yourself up to positive results.

There are simple ways for you to accomplish this. Let's start small. Take something easy. Something fun. Let's take self-care, for instance. Here is an example.

I NEED A HOBBY. IT'S TIME TO DRAIN MY BRAIN.

I have to tell you this is so very important. If you do not care for yourself and have an outlet to blow off stress, you will burn out and resent your business. Let's explore some steps using the Five Keys to Pattern Success.

Key One – Be Deliberate

Step – 01 Have a discussion with your spouse. If you are not married, pick somebody else significant in your life to be a sounding board.

Step – 02 Outline your interests and dreams and pick three activities that appeal to you.

Step – 03 Block out some time in your schedule to explore those three interests and sample the activity.

Key Two – Execute

Step – 01 Make sure you clear your schedule and make yourself unavailable for the three activities.

Step – 02 Show up and enjoy yourself.

Key Three – Analyze

Step – 01 Set up another time with your spouse or friend to discuss the three sample outings for your new hobby or activity.

Step – 02 Go out and investigate the equipment and supplies you will need to pursue this new activity.

Step – 03 Grade the expense-to-fun ratio of the new hobby or activity, and give each a score of 1–10.

Key Four – Replicate

Step – 01 Take the top two scored activities and set three blocks of time each to re-experience the new activity to see if it is sustainable and still enjoyable.

Step – 02 Prune away the activities that did not bring you as much joy or relaxation and promote the activity that did.

Step – 03 Take one quarter (3 months) to more deeply explore your new hobby and set up at least six appointments to do so.

Key Five – Systemize

Step – 01 Purchase the needed equipment for you to be successful at and enjoy your new hobby/activity.

Step – 02 Schedule a regular block of time on your schedule biweekly to enjoy and pursue your new hobby, relieving stress and recreating your best you so you can lead your team effectively.

I know you are laughing at me right now. "AC, yup, it's that easy (lol). Give me a break. Things do not just get scheduled into our lives like that." YOU ARE COMPLETELY WRONG. The fact is that is the singular reason why you have not done this already for yourself. You overcomplicate your life and procrastinate doing things for yourself. If you can't attach a revenue cycle to it, it is not important to you … is it?

I can tell you right now this is exactly how you need to achieve success in your life. Down to the smallest things. It is a pattern for you that you are not achieving what you are setting out to accomplish. OR you're so very successful in business that your personal life sucks. Do not talk yourself out of this.

I used this exact model to win the Redfish Tour National Championship my rookie season. When it happened, I was emotional and overjoyed, but I WAS NOT SURPRISED. Not everyone is a fisherman; however, if you will humor me for a few moments, I can outline a scenario in fishing that I faced that you can apply to marketing too. Watch the magic of these Five Keys.

Remember I said at the beginning of this book that fishing is not based on luck but on skill? Especially when using artificial lures and not "bait." That the phrase "The fish just were not hungry or biting today" is untrue. When was the last time you skipped a meal let alone an entire day of not eating? Fish eat every day.

When I am out fishing, I am very DELIBERATE. On my boat, I have several fishing rods and many lures in tackle boxes. There are topwater lures, diving crankbaits, soft plastic creature baits, soft plastic jerk baits, spinners, and spoons. There is no limit to the lures I have at my disposal. The key is to have an offering that I can present to the fish that gets them to commit and bite my lure.

I go into any day fishing, not with one rod or lure, but a dozen sometimes. Baitcasting reels and spinning reels. Six-foot carbon fiber rods and eight-foot fiberglass rods. Line sizes from four-pound test monofilament all the way up to thirty-pound braided line. You can see that it is easy to get overwhelmed by the options.

While on the water, I use water clarity, water temperature, the tides, solunar charts, and major and minor feeding times to pick my spot. Basically, when is dinner time, and where are the fish lining up for the buffet? I want to know where my target species is and fish there.

While pre-fishing for a tournament, I will have six to eight rods on the deck of my boat. These rods are rigged in differing configurations. Here is a list of what I might have.

Rod 01 – 1500 spinning reel, six-foot medium action rod, eight-pound braided line, six-foot twelve-pound fluorocarbon leader, snell knotted onto a 3-OT circle hook with a 3" white/glow plastic shrimp, tail hooked with a nail inserted for back weighted action.

(You can already see how detailed this gets when you're a serious angler.) I'll decrease the detail in these next rod choices.

Rod 02 – 2500 spinning reel, seven-foot, six-inch medium-fast action rod, twelve-pound braided line, fifteen-pound leader, and a jig head and paddle tail grub.

Rod 03 – 2500 baitcasting reel, seven-foot fast action rod, twelve-pound braided line, fifteen-pound leader, and a gold spoon.

For the savings of time and your sanity, if you're not an angler, I will just stick with these three combinations.

My DELIBERATE plan for today is to fish several shorelines on an incoming tide, mid-morning, for redfish. I want to target creek mouths, oyster bars, and grassy points in water depths of one foot to three feet.

My EXECUTION is to launch my boat and travel to the determined spot and start fishing these shorelines with one of the three rod and reel/bait combinations above. I arrive at my first spot, and I begin fishing.

I grab Rod 01. This is my favorite style of fishing. This is how I won the National Championship. I am partial to this rod combo and this style of fishing. It is my *thang*. I begin casting the shoreline and targeting my three targets: creek mouths, oyster bars, and grassy points.

After about fifteen minutes, I have not received a single bite. I am passionate, DELIBERATE, concentrated, and using my GO-TO technique, but no bites. So, I decide to change it up. I grab Rod 02. I start working the deeper water on the grassy points and out in front of the oyster bars. I get around 50 casts in and decide something is not working. I notice the water is a bit clouded and murky. Maybe I need some flash to draw the reds to my lure. I grab Rod Combo 03 and start chucking deep into the creek mouths and directly over and around the tops of the oyster bars in about two feet of water. Bam! I get my first hit.

I reel in that redfish and take a moment to ANALYZE the conditions under which I received my first reward.

1. I was using my spoon rod with a gold spoon.
2. I was peppering the shoreline power fishing the easily visible oyster bars and creek mouths.
3. The water depth was about two feet deep.
4. This redfish came off an oyster bar, off to the side in two feet of water on a gold spoon.

Humm, let's try that again. I start peppering the shoreline, just focusing on oyster bars in two feet of water, using my gold spoon. Ten or so casts later ... BAM! Another hit. I reel the fish in, and it is a nice twenty-six-inch redfish. I stop and ANALYZE what just happened. Have I established a pattern here?

I release the redfish I just caught, and I now switch back over to my jig pole and start targeting the same oyster bars in two feet of water to see if another bait will work. After ten or so oyster bars and about fifty casts, I do not get another bite. What is happening? Are the reds turning off? Maybe the bite is over?

I grab my spoon rod again and start power fishing the shoreline again. About fifteen casts in ... BAM! ... a hit and another redfish. Yes, I have definitely established a pattern. I repeat the use of the gold spoon now without a hook on the lure because I don't want to give all of the fish a sore mouth. I need some of these fish to still like gold spoons on tournament day. I was able to REPLICATE my result over and over again.

© SaltStrong. Image originally posted here:
https://www.saltstrong.com/articles/redfish-fishing-with-spoons/

Tournament day comes, and I load the boat up with my twelve best rod and reel combos. My best rigs based upon different scenarios. One difference is that I now have three rod and reel combos rigged with a 2500 baitcasting reel, seven-foot fast action rod, twelve-pound braided line, fifteen-pound leader, and a gold spoon. Three, so if I break a line or a reel fails, I have backups to my rod and reel combo. I have SYSTEMIZED my approach to REPLICATING the pattern I discovered during pre-tournament fishing earlier in the week.

If I flawlessly EXECUTE this pattern I discovered, I might just win this tournament. This is exactly how you handle the marketing in your business. Marketing is fishing for customers, and customers, like fish, always bite. It is never "Well, nobody is buying" or "My market is just oversaturated." It is always a matter of you dialing in your marketing to reach more potential customers, get your lure in front of them, and get them to commit/bite. It is all about you and not the fish!

If I can use these Five Keys to Pattern Success to have a great season of fishing and win a National Championship, then you can use them to win in business and in your personal life. Remember, this is how I met and married my Redhead, and we are living happily ever after.

CHAPTER 20

IT IS ALL IN YOUR HANDS

Listen, I don't want you to tattoo this on your hand. I do want to burn this into your heart. It is up to you now to take these tools and REPLICATE success over and over again in your life. This is a simple system for extraordinary results.

I use these Five Keys to build multimillion-dollar businesses. The exact systems outlined in this book. These are not quaint little examples; they are powerful explosive harbingers of truth that will elevate your performance as they did mine. They are tried and true and, as I mentioned before, gravitational.

Gravitational concepts are those that are elemental in truth. They are like gravity. You cannot argue with gravity. Nobody fights over the validity of gravity. We all know if you jump off a bridge, you're not going flying. You're going swimming. Gravitational concepts always work and are always true.

Faith is an ingredient you will need. Faith, by meaning, is to act on something you cannot see or understand. I am asking you to step out in faith and start using these keys right away. Strip everything you have come to believe about accomplishing goals and becoming successful away for a time. Focus on the flow of Being DELIBERATE and having a plan. EXECUTING without procrastination. Taking time out to ANALYZE your returns. Pruning away the unfruitful and doubling down on the positive results through REPLICATION. Then building SYSTEMS that self-perpetuate that REPLICATION, turning your results into a reliable, sustainable, rewarding business.

You will have haters, detractors, demons, and the like that will not be happy you are winning. It is the "crabs in the bucket" syndrome. One crab fights its way to the top of the bucket to escape its demise, all while the other crabs grab and claw at the escaping crab, pulling it back down to meet its death. Everyone is designed for success, but few ever decide to honor that God-given engineering.

Success is but a mirror. To some, it reflects confirmation, affirming the correct steps they are taking towards their goals. To others, it reflects their laziness, confirming their lack of commitment and failings. Once you begin to get traction and success becomes evident, you will begin to gleam and shine, reflecting on those in your sphere of influence. Your success will breathe hope into some people's lives or speak despair into others. You will need to choose who you want to fellowship with. Those of hope or those of despair.

You are going to need to run with a new herd. Are you going to be a schoolie bass or a lunker bass? You see, schoolie bass run around the lake in schools all day,

It Is All In Your Hands

chasing minnows. In the school, one bass does not stand out from the next bass. All of the bass are sixteen inches long, two pounds each, and shaped like footballs. As schoolie bass swim along in the school, they look to the left and the right, comparing themselves to their schoolie friends. They say to themselves, "I'm fat and happy. I am sixteen inches long, just like all of my friends. I weigh two pounds. I am shaped like a football. I must have arrived."

Schoolie bass swim all over the wide-open expanses of the lake, chasing minnows for food. Their energy output pursuing minnows is great. Once they catch and consume a minnow, the caloric reward of eating that minnow is just more than the calories spent chasing and catching that minnow. Though schoolie bass are schooling, swimming, chasing, and eating minnows continuously, their reward is small in comparison. Therefore, the schoolie bass take years to reach the length of sixteen inches, the weight of two pounds, shaped like a football benchmark, and stay there forever.

In contrast, lunker bass are smart and sly. They conserve energy. They are solitary, largely living by themselves and having few friends. The schoolie bass don't understand the lunker bass and tease them. They get in their schools, mock the lunker bass, and show off to their buddies who are just like them. They do not understand the ways of the lunker bass and criticize them.

What the lunker bass knows is that along the edge of the lake, where it's weedy and dense, where it's hard to free swim, leap and frolic, there is a crawfish superhighway. Every day, crawfish travel up and down this crawfish superhighway, doing crawfish stuff. Along this superhighway, there are weed banks and logs. Perfect ambush spots for Mr. Lunker Bass.

The lunker bass will find a log and lay in wait for a fat, juicy, calorie-laden crawfish to move down the crawfish superhighway across the front of the lunker bass's log. You see, what that lunker bass knows is that a crawfish is a good meal and a meal that will last you a long time. In a flash, with minimal calories consumed, a lunker bass can pounce from its lair behind the log next to the crawfish superhighway and slurp up a fat, juicy crawfish.

The lunker bass knows that the calories expended for pouncing out to catch that crawfish are minimal compared to the jackpot of calorie rewards eating that juicy crawfish will give them. In fact, that lunker bass only needs to consume but a few calorie-laden crawfish in a single day compared to the hundreds of minnows a single schoolie bass will need to consume to survive.

It's sad because the schoolie bass never realize their potential. You see, schoolie bass and lunker bass are made from the same genetic material. It is at some point when the bass are juveniles, they decide to either join the school or dig into the undergrowth of the edges of the lake. At any time, a schoolie bass can leave the school and choose the edge waters of the lake and do what lunker bass do, but the familiarity of the school keeps them from wanting more.

Lunker bass reach their true potential because they are not afraid of the hard choices and see the lake as a multi-dimensional body of water to explore and harvest from. Lunker bass have surely eaten a few minnows in their time, but they have never relied solely upon them for forage. Lunker bass learn and grow, sampling from many areas of the lake, and they learn the careful dance of calories expended versus calories consumed. Lunker bass become what they were engineered to be and do not stave off that opportunity.

My question to you is: What kind of bass do you want to be? A schoolie bass or a lunker bass?

Yes, this is a red pill/blue pill question. Do you want to go on in life now knowing that success is a REPLICABLE, SYSTEMIZED recipe? Or do you want to get plugged back into the school and have your mind erased of these few hours you have spent with me? Do you want to be a lunker bass?

"But AC, I don't know where to start" – Be DELIBERATE
"AC, I am afraid I won't succeed" – EXECUTE
"I am lazy and don't like math" – ANALYZE
Prune away the underperforming – REPLICATE
"I don't have a lot of time, I have a family" – SYSTEMIZE

You can do it. I have faith in you. Get ready for success. Wear it well. Realize your full potential and blessings from GOD.

The Lord bless you and keep you.
The Lord make his face to shine upon you,
and be gracious unto you.
The Lord turn his face towards you,
and give you peace.
(Numbers 6:24–26)

Blessings upon you. Go forth and prosper.

THE LEGEND OF THE HUMMINGBIRD AND THE FOREST FIRE

Some time ago, a horrible forest fire broke out, consuming everything in its path. All of the habitats of the resident animals were viciously ravaged and destroyed by the fire. As the animals fled for their lives, they found themselves encircled by the fire's rage and were backed up against the ocean with no escape.

Suddenly, a tiny hummingbird broke from the fire, buzzing towards the ocean. Darting in and out from the fire, the other animals took notice. This little hummingbird was frantically flying out to meet the waters and slurping the most minuscule amount of water into its fragile beak, buzzing back to drop the water onto the fire.

The other animals questioned the hummingbird, "What are you doing?" The hummingbird replied, "I am trying to put out the forest fire and save our homes."

Many of the animals began to mock the tiny hummingbird and tease him. Others questioned the viability of his plan, saying "What possible difference can you make? You are just a small hummingbird with a tiny beak."

The hummingbird replied, "I am doing all I can. Maybe if we all run back and forth from the ocean carrying water to the fire, we can extinguish the flames and save our homes."

And they did. All of the animals worked together, lapping up small amounts of water, spewing it out upon the flames, and they saved the forest. All from the example of the one small hummingbird that knew it had to do something to make a difference, no matter how small or seemingly insignificant.

My life, I live in service to you, setting an example, not in vain conceit but rather in inspiration to you. I hope that by buzzing around like this little hummingbird, I will lead you to join me in making a larger impact for those God has entrusted to us.

ACKNOWLEDGEMENTS

How can you write a first book and keep your dedications to but a few? If you have accomplished anything in your life and are truly humble about your success, you know that you did not get to the summit of the mountain alone. Acknowledging that, allow me to thank a few.

First, to my wife Karen. No wife of an entrepreneur truly understands the ride they are about to set out on. My wife has been understanding when I dream and reach far beyond my personal abilities. She has supported me through the desolate and unsustainable times of business reimagination. Where no amount of money could ever pay for the time and attention she has had to invest in serving me. She encouraged me (in her sassy redheaded Texan way), talking through steps and affirming my decisions, filling in the gaps where I skipped right over important steps. She is my rock, my true love, and my soulmate. The greatest business and life partner I could ever ask for.

To my father. The truth is, if you have never been at odds with your father, you really never had a father. Only a few have the blessing of having a father who is hard on them. My father never had the chance to have an adult relationship with his father. His father, my grandfather, passed from this earth while my father was still young. Though my father and I struggled later in life, he was my best teacher, my first mentor, my hardest coach, a fishing buddy, and a catalyst for change in my life. I would not be where I am today if it were not for my dad. Through the good times and bad in our relationship, I have now come to realize that even in our darkest hours and deepest conflicts, his actions drove me towards success, often kicking and screaming.

I can now look back at the entirety of our relationship and see that it is weighted far in the good/win column. I have matured to see that it was God moving through him to push me to the sweet spot, the place where I would have the most significance.

Thank you, Dad. There would be no AC Lockyer without AL Lockyer.

Padre Dan Holland. I listened to your lessons Sunday mornings for 25 years as my pastor. Those lessons from the Bible have your wisdom and flare packed into them. These words helped guide me to be a true Christian Businessman, understanding there was no compartmentalization between family, church, and business. There was only life as a Christ-follower, and my business was an extension of that. You and your wife Beth became close friends with Karen and me. Later, you came on board to help lead my businesses. You saw my value early and affirmed me when my path was not clear. Thank you for doing life with me and being a frank and loyal friend.

To all of those who saw my value early and encouraged me to reach higher and not settle for average.

My Future Farmers of America Ag teachers, Mr. Freeze and Mr. Lawson, you coached me to step up into leadership and called me higher as a young man.

Thresher Klier, you were my cheerleader and biggest fan when I had the dream to become a professional fisherman and stepped in to support that dream as my fishing partner. Always the calm voice of reason, you stood there on that poling platform and let me be me, sucking up the oxygen and competing for a championship. Which we won together as a team.

Kevin Hipes and Roy Reid, for standing alongside me and encouraging me as I reinvented myself after a bad family business breakup. Roy, especially your spiritual gift of keeping up with our relationship and keeping us connected. Always checking in to hear about the latest news and give me direction along my path.

Without these and many, many more, I would not be here writing this book today. So many I cannot mention. I can think of at least thirty, off-the-top-of-my-head, that have influenced my path and made me better. If you are one of those who went unmentioned, I sincerely apologize. I could not mention everyone. In my heart and yours, you know your special place, even though you go unmentioned in this manuscript. Thank you one and all.

Finally and most importantly, to my Lord and Christ Jesus who makes all things possible. Thank you for giving me focus and purpose to what I do every day, and for allowing me to participate in God's perfect plan for this earth as a vessel to bless others in His will.

CPSIA information can be obtained
at www.ICGtesting.com
Printed in the USA
BVHW041103260322
632228BV00003B/9/J